HQ
728
R388
1990

41.00

D1175671

WITHDRAWN

Media Center (Library)
ELIZABETHTOWN COMMUNITY COLLEGE
Elizabethtown, KY 42701

The Retreat From Marriage

The Rockford Institute

The purpose of The Rockford Institute is to rebuild an American ethical consensus rooted in the fundamental ideas and traditions of Western civilization. Through research, conferences, and publications, the Institute seeks to influence the moral and intellectual forces that shape social and cultural trends and public issues. The Institute has programs in the general areas of religion and society, the family, and literature. It is a non-profit, tax-exempt educational organization.

Publications

Chronicles: A Magazine of American Culture — A monthly magazine that considers the influence of ideas, arts, and letters upon the character and viability of American society.

The Family in America — In-depth analysis each month of a topic of long-range importance to the family and democratic capitalism; includes news and information.

The Religion & Society Report — A monthly newsletter surveying events, trends, and publications across the religious spectrum that influence American culture and public issues.

Main St. Memorandum — A quarterly newsletter of Institute achievements for contributors and friends, contains important Op-Ed placements.

Communication

Institute research is especially adapted for newspaper editorial pages. Articles have appeared recently in The Wall Street Journal, USA Today, The Los Angeles Times, The Washington Post, the Chicago Tribune, the Chicago Sun-Times, the Houston Chronicle, and numerous other newspapers throughout the country. Staff articles have appeared in The Public Interest, Policy Review, Regulation, The American Spectator, Reason, and other journals of scholarship and opinion. Talk-show appearances by Institute staff include CBS Nightly News, NBC News, ABC's Nightline, William Buckley's Firing Line, CNN, CBN's 700 Club, National Public Radio, and numerous local television and radio programs.

Administration

Allan C. Carlson, president of the Institute; Michael Y. Warder, executive vice president; Bryce J. Christensen, director of the Institute Center on the Family in America, editor of The Family in America; Thomas J. Fleming, editor of Chronicles; John A. Howard, counselor to the Institute and director of the Ingersoll program; and Harold O.J. Brown, director of The Center on Religion & Society, editor of The Religion & Society Report.

Board of Directors

William Andrews (Chairman), William Nelson (Vice Chairman), Allan Carlson, Clayton Gaylord, Mary Kohler, Robert Krieble, Norman P. McClelland, Dallin Oaks, George O'Neill, Jr., Henry Regnery, Robert Sandblom, Clyde Sluhan, James Bond Stockdale, Kathleen M. Sullivan, Katherine M. Swim, Frederick G. Wacker, Jr., Robert L. Woodson.

For more information:

Michael Warder, executive vice president; The Rockford Institute, 934 North Main Street, Rockford, Illinois 61103 (815) 964-5811.

The Retreat From Marriage
Causes and Consequences

Edited by
Bryce J. Christensen

UNIVERSITY
PRESS OF
AMERICA

nham • New York • London

THE FAMILY
IN AMERICA

RESEARCH SERIES

The Rockford Institute

Copyright © 1990 by
University Press of America®, Inc.
4720 Boston Way
Lanham, Maryland 20706

3 Henrietta Street
London WC2E 8LU England

All rights reserved
Printed in the United States of America
British Cataloging in Publication Information Available

Co-published by arrangement with
The Rockford Institute

Library of Congress Cataloging-in-Publication Data

The Retreat from marriage : causes and consequences /
edited by Bryce J. Christensen.
p.   cm.
Papers from a conference convened by the Rockford
Institute Center on the Family in America together
with summaries of the discussions.
Includes index.
1. Marriage—United States—Congresses.
2. Family—United States—Congresses.
I. Christensen, Bryce J.   II. Rockford Institute.
Center on the Family in America.
HQ728.R388   1990   306.8—dc20   90–42278 CIP

ISBN 0–8191–7897–7 (alk. paper)
ISBN 0–8191–7898–5 (pbk)

 The paper used in this publication meets the minimum requirements of
American National Standard for Information Sciences—Permanence
of Paper for Printed Library Materials, ANSI Z39.48–1984.

Contents

Acknowledgments

The Rockford Institute wishes to express appreciation to The Joyce Foundation of Chicago, Illinois, for its generous support for the conference on "The Retreat From Marriage."

Preface

Wedding bells ring less often now than in the past. Fewer Americans are choosing to marry; those who do marry later in life. The first-marriage rate among unmarried women ages 15 to 44 has fallen over 30 percent since 1970. The average age for first marriage has climbed to almost 27 for men and to 24.5 for women. One American in eight now remains unmarried for life. Meanwhile, the divorce courts keep busy terminating many of those marriages that do form. Between 40 and 50 percent of all marriages (including remarriages) occurring in the 1980's will probably end in divorce. No wonder the percentage of American children born out of wedlock has risen from about 4 percent of all births in 1950 to over 20 percent in the mid 1980's.

What is causing this retreat from marriage? Why in any case does it matter? Some observers, convinced that family decisions are merely matters of personal preference, view the recent changes without concern. Indeed, because they regard marriage as a form of patriarchal oppression, some feminists actually welcome the rise of single and nontraditional lifestyles. Unmarried motherhood attracts particular attention as a lifestyle involving a swelling number of Americans. Although almost one American baby in four is now born out of wedlock, divorce figures as an important cause of the remarkable decline in American fertility — "the birth dearth." Each year divorce also pushes about a million of America's children into single-parent households, most of them headed by women. Relatively few Americans feel much enthusiasm for single-parent households. Compared to children in intact homes, children in single-parent households are more likely to live in poverty, to suffer from poor health, to fail in school, to end up in jail, or to be committed to a mental institution.

Unmarried men and women themselves suffer from a host of psychological, medical, and economic problems that strike their married peers less often. In general, married men and women express greater satisfaction with their lives than do the unmarried. The unmarried and the married differ in more than their subjective well-being. Much of the purported "gender gap" in American politics is actually a "marriage gap": while married men and women vote alike in presidential elections, unmarried women show a distinctive preference for Democratic candidates. Unmarried mothers — many of whom depend upon the state as a surrogate spouse — are far more likely than married women or men to support liberal and leftist candidates for office.

Hoping to foster clearer thinking on these issues, The Rockford Institute Center on the Family in America convened a research conference on "The Retreat from Marriage," calling together 16 scholars, writers, and analysts for an extended discussion of the issues. The sessions of the conference each focused on a major paper, all four of which are published here. But the group discussion — published here in summary form — explores many issues barely touched upon in the papers.

The conference participants all expressed concern about the statistical trends (examined here in some detail), but heated disagreements soon erupted over how to interpret these trends and about how to shape future public policies affecting family life. Several in attendance stressed the importance of shifting moral attitudes in shaping family life. Others disputed this line of argument, emphasizing instead new technological and economic pressures. Some blamed industrial capitalism for the decay of family life; others indicted the welfare state. Divided by sharp disagreement about the welfare state, participants turned their attention to the broader question of how modern ideologies — particularly feminism and utopianism — have affected family life. The shadow of ideology fell not only on the conference's primary topic (marriage), but on several secondary ones as well, including "no fault" divorce, child support, abortion, female employment, and day care.

As the conference moved toward its conclusion, participants contemplated the future. Some voiced despair, interpreting family decline as a symptom of impending cultural collapse. Others dismissed the jeremiads as a distraction from the immediate task of devising specific public policies for strengthening family life. Still, even some of the optimists acknowledged the need for a moral renewal to fortify the home. But is religion the only possible source of such a renewal? Do Americans need some kind of catastrophe to shock them into a reassessment of their moral outlook? Readers will find at least as many questions as answers in this book. But if this volume provokes serious reflection upon such questions, it will fulfill its intent.

— *Bryce J. Christensen*
Rockford, Illinois
October 1989

Current Trends in Nonmarital Fertility and Divorce

by Herbert L. Smith

T he "retreat from marriage" presumably takes many paths — postponement of marriage, cohabitation, abjuration of traditional roles within marriage, and more. But if we ask "What is making the retreat from marriage look more like a rout?" then our focus is brought to bear on trends in two aspects of social and demographic behavior. The first is nonmarital fertility, which removes the quintessential family function — reproduction — from two-parent families. The second is divorce, a conscious rejection of a specific marriage, if not of marriage as an institution.[1]

This paper provides an overview of recent trends in nonmarital fertility and divorce in the United States. The social acts involved — sexual activity, marriage, divorce — are generally deemed to be forms of adult behavior, and most measures of these activities focus on their prevalence in the adult population. But both nonmarital fertility and divorce have as potential consequences the disruption of the lives of children, and the extent of this disruption and disadvantage is not always apparent from statistics calculated for adults. Thus, where possible, I report parallel measures from the standpoint of children.

Also where possible, my exposition of trends distinguishes between those for whites and those for blacks (or nonwhites). This is always possible with regard to nonmarital fertility, but divorce statistics are rarely race specific. There are several reasons for discussing blacks and whites separately. First, the U.S. white and black subpopulations are demographically distinct from one another. Intermarriage and procreation across racial lines are comparatively rare (Lieberson and Waters 1988, chapter 6). Second, levels and trends of demographic behavior such as nonmarital fertility (and, in some respects, divorce) differ considerably between whites and blacks. Third, it has been suggested (although the point can be contested) that "the changes in family structure that occurred among blacks are a leading indicator of what may happen among whites" (Farley 1988, p. 491). The disadvantage of maintaining distinctions between the American white and black subpopulations is the reification of invidious comparisons based on an ascriptive social characteristic.

The organization of this paper is simple. I first present trends in nonmarital fertility, then trends in divorce. There is no explicit attempt to link the two. Marital disruption — divorce, in particular — places women in a status where they are "at risk" of a nonmarital pregnancy and birth, but most children born out of wedlock are born to women who have never married.[2] Implicitly, however, they are linked by common causes — some of which are discussed briefly at the conclusion of the paper — and common consequences for children and future generations.

Trends in Nonmarital Fertility

The Vital Statistics of the United States (National Center for Health Statistics 1988b) reported 933,013 out of wedlock births in 1987 — a figure slightly less than the population of Rhode Island, but greater than the populations of Montana, Vermont, North Dakota, South Dakota, Delaware, or Alaska (U.S. Bureau of the Census 1989, p. 22) and well in excess of the population required for a congressional seat. Figure 1 shows the steady growth in the number of nonmarital births annually for the period 1940-1986. There were 100,000 such births per annum by 1944, 200,000 by 1957, 400,000 by 1971, and 800,000 by 1985. This doubling every 13 or 14 years coincides with an annualized growth rate of 5%. In comparison, marital births (also shown in Figure 1) peaked in the late 1950's and early 1960's at just over 4,000,000 per annum and thereupon declined to under 3,000,000 per annum in every year since 1972. Absent nonmarital fertility, there is no "echo" to the post-war "baby boom." Growth in the sheer number of nonmarital births is only a part of the picture, however. Such numbers depend on the size of the population at risk — nonmarried women of child-bearing age — and potentially mask significant differentials by race and age.

There are two standard measures of nonmarital fertility. The first is the *nonmarital fertility rate*, also known as the illegitimacy rate or the out of wedlock birth rate. It is calculated as the ratio of the number of births *both* conceived and delivered out of wedlock in a year's time to the mid-year population of unmarried women

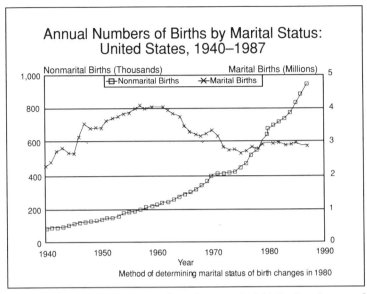

Figure 1. Since 1940, the number of nonmarital births has increased exponentially; marital births peaked at four million circa 1960, and now number under three million annually.

(times 1,000) for a specific age. The general nonmarital fertility rate is the number of out of wedlock births per 1,000 women ages 15-44, but other rates specific to smaller age intervals are also routinely calculated, and some of these are shown below. This "legal" definition of nonmarital fertility excludes births conceived out of wedlock but legitimated via marriage prior to delivery, as well as births conceived in marriage but delivered after the marriage has dissolved. Jones *et al.* (1985) consider the effects of an alternative "social" definition of nonmarital fertility — one that includes all births delivered out of wedlock, irrespective of the mother's marital status at conception, and includes births occurring while the mother's marriage is in separation as out of wedlock as well — on nonmarital fertility rates. They find that over the period 1968-1977, socially defined out of wedlock births exceed legally defined out of wedlock births by anywhere from a third to a sixth, with the gap narrowing toward the end of this period (Jones *et al.* 1985, Figure 1, p. 685). Shifting from a legal to a social

definition of nonmarital fertility adds a higher proportion of nonmarital births to the white population than it does to the black
population, thereby attenuating (but by no means eliminating)
black-white differences in nonmarital fertility. Unfortunately, the
detailed micro-level data necessary to transform the traditional
(legally defined) rates of nonmarital fertility into rates based on the
more inclusive social definition are not available for as long a span
of time, and thus all rates considered here are based on the
traditional definition.

The second standard measure of nonmarital fertility is the
nonmarital fertility ratio, also known as the illegitimacy ratio or
the out of wedlock birth ratio. The nonmarital fertility ratio is the
proportion (per 1,000) of births in a given year both conceived and
delivered out of wedlock. See Jones *et al.* (1985) for an investigation
of the effects of a social definition of nonmarital fertility on these
ratios. In spite of their similar names, the nonmarital fertility ratio
and the nonmarital fertility rate are fundamentally different
entities. The nonmarital fertility rate is a function of the sexual
activity, contraceptive use (including efficacy), recourse to abortion, and extent of legitimation via marriage among nonmarried
women (Cutright and Smith 1988) — regardless of their number in
the population. In contrast, nonmarital fertility ratios, since they
are specific to births, not women at risk of births, are functions of
all of the foregoing *plus* rates of fertility among *married* women and
the relative distribution of married and nonmarried women in the
population (Smith and Cutright 1988). It is thus a logical possibility for nonmarital fertility rates to go down, but the nonmarital
fertility ratio to go up (or vice versa), owing to more rapid declines
in marital fertility and/or shifts in the relative distribution of the
female childbearing population, from married to nonmarried. The
empirical reality of this surface conundrum has been documented,
specifically for the U.S. black population, by Espenshade (1985),
Jones *et al.* (1985), and Smith and Cutright (1988).

Given both the possibility and fact of divergent trends in nonmarital fertility conditional on the demographic measure employed, it is important that recourse to one or the other be based on
substantive considerations, not habit or happenstance. Elsewhere
(Smith and Cutright 1988, pp. 236-237) I have argued that the
underlying conceptual distinction between the two measures is
generation-based and best motivated with respect to the *conse-*

quences of nonmarital fertility. If interest is focused on the consequences of being an unmarried mother (which admittedly subsumes a larger set of women than those giving birth out of wedlock alone), then relevant trends are those indexed by nonmarital fertility rates, which can loosely be interpreted as (age-specific) probabilities that a nonmarried woman will have a child.[3] If interest is focused on the life chances of cohorts of children born out of wedlock, relative to those born into intact marriages, then the nonmarital fertility ratio is the appropriate statistic. Because generations of children are not socially differentiated to any great degree by age of mother, nonmarital fertility ratios specific to age of mother at birth are of no great moment and, hence, are not considered here. Thus, if we seek to answer the question, "What is happening with teenage childbearing in the U.S.?" we consult trends in the nonmarital fertility rate of 15 to 19 year olds. If, on the other hand, we wish to know the proportion of school children who will have been born out of wedlock, it is the nonmarital fertility ratio that is most relevant.

All figures in the ensuing subsections (plus Figure 1, above) are based on data from the Vital Statistics of the United States. There is a break at 1980, coinciding with a shift in methods of estimating versus inferring nonmarried births. See the Technical Appendix of National Center for Health Statistics (1988b) for further details. Data for blacks, as opposed to nonwhites, are available beginning in 1969 only.

Nonmarital Fertility Rates

Figure 2 presents nonmarital fertility rates by race for the United States for the period 1940-1987.[4] Nonwhite fertility rates rose dramatically in the first two decades of this interval to an apparent peak in 1961. Since then they have declined by approximately 20%, although the drop has not been smooth. There are notable "upticks" around 1970, again in the late 1970's, and during the last three years for which data are available, 1985-1987. In contrast, white nonmarital fertility rates, although far lower than those of blacks, have been steadily increasing. The rate of increase was nowhere near as great over the period 1940 to 1960 as it was among blacks, but then neither was there a post-1960 decline. The temporary dip in rates in the early 1970's *may* be related to liberalization of abortion laws, culminating with the *Roe* v. *Wade* decision in 1973.

(It also coincides with an even steeper drop in black rates during the first half of the 1970's, but this is less compelling evidence since blacks were [and are] far less likely than whites to undergo abortions [Nathanson and Kim 1989; Henshaw 1987].) Similarly, the 1985-1987 increase in rates for both blacks and whites is *suggestive* of the effects of recent restrictions in governmental funding of abortions for the poor.

The divergence in rates between whites and nonwhites from

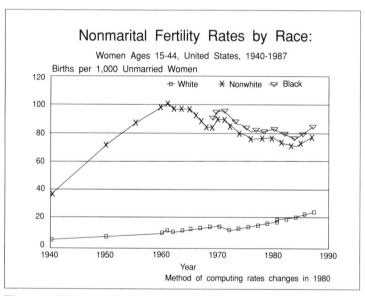

Figure 2. The nonwhite nonmarital fertility rate declined substantially during the 1960s and 70s, while the white rate has climbed to new highs during the 1980s

1940 to 1960, coupled with their post-1960 convergence, results in the dip in the curve shown in Figure 3 for the percentage of nonmarital births which are white. In 1946, nonwhite rates exceeded white rates in a ratio roughly equivalent to the inverse of the ratio of nonmarried women of childbearing age in the two subpopulations, so that 49% of all births out of wedlock occurred to whites. As nonwhite nonmarital fertility rates grew — far faster than either white nonmarital fertility rates or relative increases in the nonwhite population — this percentage shrank to 35% in 1956. Since then, the percentage of out of wedlock births occurring to whites has grown steadily, passing the 50% mark in 1983 and reaching 53% in 1986 and 1987. Although nonmarital fertility rates are still far higher among nonwhites than among whites, out of wedlock births are now more numerous among whites than among blacks.

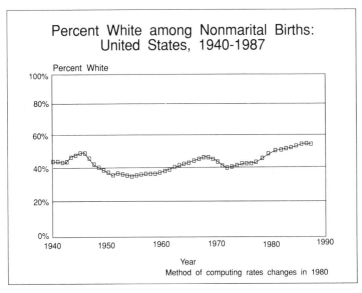

Figure 3. Between 1956 and 1986, the proportion of nonmarital births in the U.S. that were white grew from 35% to 53%.

Trends in general nonmarital fertility rates such as those shown in Figure 2 are subject to variability owing to change in the age structure of each subpopulation. Nonmarital fertility rates are higher at some ages (late teens and early to mid 20's) than others (30's and 40's), and so as a population ages, general nonmarital fertility rates may fall even without change in age-specific rates. Similarly, changes in the age at marriage and/or the prevalence of divorce may shift the age distribution of nonmarried women in such a way as to alter rates of nonmarital fertility absent change in underlying age-specific rates. For these reasons, as well as an intrinsic interest in more detailed trends, we turn now to the examination of age-specific rates by race. Nonmarital fertility rates for whites are shown in Figure 4. Comparable data for nonwhites are displayed in Figure 5 and for blacks — from 1969 only — in Figure 6. Rates are specific to five-year age intervals, although after 1965 it is possible to break teenage fertility into rates for 15-17 and 18-19 year olds, and prior to 1969, 35-39 year olds and 40-44 year olds must be grouped together.

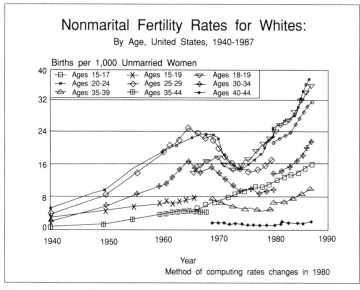

Figure 4. Rapid increases at all ages during the 1980s have returned white nonmarital fertility rates to levels at or above previous post-war highs.

The most salient feature of Figures 4 through 6 — and something that is not evident in the general nonmarital fertility rates shown in Figure 2 — is the great volatility in rates among whites since the mid-1960's and the comparative constancy of nonwhite rates during the same interval.[5] The latter is particularly evident in Figure 6 for blacks, where the perspective is from 1969 onward. Rates for blacks among almost all age groups declined slightly in the early 1970's and have changed very little since. The 1985-1987 uptick is evident at all ages from 18 through 35, but not among 15-17 year olds.

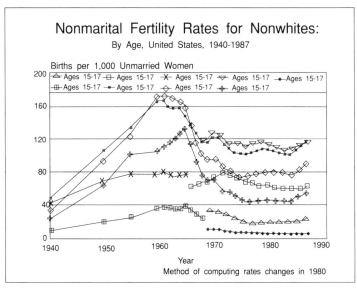

Figure 5. Nonmarital fertility rates for nonwhites at all ages declined during the 1960s, and have been relatively stable since then.

Trends in nonwhite (black) nonmarital fertility can be usefully summarized with four observations. (1) These rates are high. Unmarried black women ages 18-19 have fertility rates equivalent to 80% of the fertility rates of *married* women ages 25-29 — both white and black. (2) However, nonwhite nonmarital fertility rates are not especially high in historical perspective. Adult rates as of 1987 are far lower than they were 25 years earlier. (3) Nor are these rates uniquely high in comparative perspective. Nonmarital fertility rates at ages 35-39 and 40-44 in Australia were higher than those which obtained among U.S. nonwhites during the 1970's and into the early 1980's; nonmarital fertility rates in England and Wales circa 1968 for 30-34 year olds were essentially equivalent to those prevailing among same-aged U.S. nonwhites in the early 1980's (Cutright and Smith 1986). (4) Nonmarital fertility among blacks is sometimes said to have reached epidemic proportions. This is an inappropriate metaphor. An epidemic implies contagion and escalation; if there was an epidemic, it peaked 25 years ago (Vinovskis 1988). This is also true with respect to nonwhite teenage fertility, which did not reach a comparable crest in the early 1960's: There is no evidence of any "epidemic" increase in teenage fertility going back at least 30 years. Even as marriage prospects have waxed and waned, the underlying propensity to have a birth out of wedlock has remained remarkably steady. There has, however, been some increase in black nonmarital fertility rates post-1984, especially at ages 18-29. Whether this presages a transition to higher levels of nonmarital fertility rates remains to be seen.

If there is an epidemic, it is occurring among whites. Figure 4 shows that adult nonmarital fertility (nonmarital childbearing to women ages 20-44) peaked in the mid to late 1960's, then returned in the 1970's to levels equivalent to those that had prevailed twenty

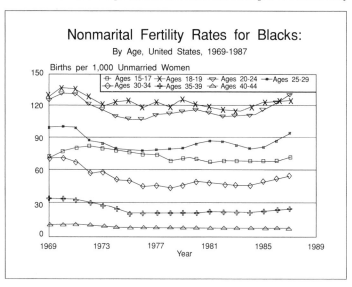

Figure 6. Black nonmarital fertility rates have changed very little since the mid-1970s, although there has been an upturn post-1984, especially among ages 18-29.

years earlier. Rates have since boomed again, especially at ages 20-34, and it appears that white nonmarital fertility rates as of 1987 are as high as they have ever been.[6] Although the curves for each age group are by no means identical, they are very similar, and such deviations in the timing of peaks and troughs as do occur are *not* staggered at five-year intervals, as would be the case if temporal variation in nonmarital fertility had a birth cohort-specific component, as suggested by Easterlin (1980, pp. 89-93; *cf.* Cutright and Smith 1986).

Among white teenagers, the trend is ever upward. Among 18-19 year olds, there is some evidence of a late-1960's peak, but in any event it is quite minor, representing only a small deviation from an otherwise accelerating trend. Nonmarital fertility among 15-17 year-old white girls has risen steadily and linearly since 1966, the first date when detailed age-specific data are available. The extent to which teenage nonmarital fertility followed a different trend in the recent past is exemplified by a comparison of 18-19 and 20-24 year old rates. In 1966, 18-19 year-old rates lagged those of 20-24 year olds by approximately one-third. But because there was no decline in teenage rates during the early 1970's comparable to that which occurred in the early 1970's, these rates soon converged and have moved in virtual lockstep for over a decade. Whereas there is no age group among nonwhites which has not previously seen far higher rates of nonmarital fertility than those currently extant, nonmarital fertility rates among 18-24 year-old (young, typically never-married) whites as of 1987 were as high as those which had *ever* obtained among *any* age group of white women. Herein may lie some of the explanation for the great attention focused of late on nonmarital childbearing.

Further discussion of differences in nonmarital fertility by age and by race will be abetted by more attention to age- and race-specific trends in the proximate determinants of nonmarital fertility: exposure to intercourse and extent of sexual activity; contraceptive use, including efficacy; resort to abortion; and the likelihood of marriage prior to birth given a premarital conception (Cutright 1971). Four reasons why rates of nonmarital fertility are higher among blacks than among whites are (1) blacks initiate intercourse at an earlier age and are more likely to be sexually active than are whites (Zelnick and Kantner 1980); (2) blacks are less likely than whites to contracept (Tanfer and Horn 1985; Hofferth and Hayes 1987); (3) blacks are less likely than whites to abort a nonmarital pregnancy (Henshaw 1987); and (4) blacks are less likely than whites to legitimate an out of wedlock conception (Jones *et al.* 1985). Such black-white differences do, however, differ in magnitude by age. In 1980, differences in sexual activity and in the probability of legitimation each accounted for a third of the black-white differential in the rate of births conceived out of wedlock among teenagers, but only a fifth each of the same differential among 25-29 year olds. Conversely, differential contraceptive use accounted for only a tenth of the black-white difference in this rate among teenagers, but a fifth among women in their late 20's. Only the effect of the greater reluctance of nonmarried blacks to seek abortions was constant over age, explaining approximately 30% of the race differential in rates of out of wedlock conception (Cutright and Smith 1988).

These results are, however, specific to a single year and beg the question of how *change* in such factors affects change in the rates reviewed above. Fortunately, there is an increasing amount of data on the trends in the proximate determinants of nonmarital fertility, especially for teenagers, sufficient to sustain decompositions of intertemporal variability of nonmarital fertility rates. Hofferth, Kahn, and Baldwin (1987) document how premarital sexual activity of teenagers increased dramatically during the 1970's when "there occurred a major transformation in sexual behavior in the United States" (p. 46). The percentage of teenage women who had ever had premarital sexual intercourse rose from approximately 30% to 40% among whites and approximately 50% to 60% among blacks. The average age at first intercourse declined as well. *Ceteris paribus*, such changes in the number of unmarried teens at risk of becoming pregnant might have been expected to raise nonmarried fertility rates. As we have seen, rates for white teens did increase substantially during the 1970's. But black teen rates did not, which calls our attention to the respective roles of contraception, abortion, and legitimation through marriage in mitigating the effects of increased exposure to intercourse. Nathanson and Kim (1989) show that approximately half of the increase among whites in probabilities of premarital teenage births was accounted for by the aforementioned increase in premarital sexual activity, and another quarter each by increases in rates of pregnancy among the sexually active (*i.e.*, nonuse or poor use of contraception, or greater frequency of intercourse) and probabilities of nonmarital births given the occurrence of a pregnancy (although abortion increased, legitimation of premarital conceptions declined even more). Among black teenagers, increases in sexual activity were compensated for by declines in rates of pregnancy given intercourse (better contraception) and nonmarital births given premarital pregnancy (chiefly because of more recourse to abortion; rates of legitimation — already low — continued to decline).

Table 1. White teenagers are far more likely than black teenagers to either abort a premarital pregnancy or legitimate it through marriage. But legitimation dropped precipitously for both groups during the 1970's.

Percentage Distribution of Nonmarital Pregnancy Outcomes
of
Metropolitan U.S. Teenagers by Race, 1971 and 1979

Pregnancy Outcome

Race	Year	Marry before pregnancy outcome	Abortion	Live birth	Total[a]	(n)[b]
White	1971	51.3%	23.4	25.3	100.0%	(1,758)
	1979	20.3%	47.1	32.7	100.1%	(981)
Black	1971	8.5%	12.8	78.7	100.0%	(1,034)
	1979	4.3%	25.0	70.8	100.1%	(683)

Notes: [a]Totals may not sum to 100.0% due to rounding.

[b]Denominators (n's) are as reported in source text. The actual n's on which these percentages are based may be somewhat lower.

Source: Nathanson and Kim (1989, Table 3).

Table 1 presents race-specific distributions of nonmarital pregnancy outcomes in both 1971 and 1979. Among white teenagers in 1971, approximately half of all premarital conceptions were legitimated and a quarter were aborted, whereas by 1979, these proportions were virtually reversed. Among blacks, the already small proportion of such births legitimated was halved, while the proportion of abortions doubled. Of particular note is the decline in marriage as an option given a premarital pregnancy. The odds of abortion rather than legitimation, averaged across both groups, rose five-fold; the odds of a premarital birth rather than a legitimating marriage rose almost three-fold. Vinovskis and Chase-Lansdale (1987) argue that this rapid decline was fostered in large part by "expert" social science opinion that discouraged teenage marriage. Furstenburg (1988), however, points out that declines in teenage marriages — marriages often precipitated by a premarital pregnancy — actually began in the 1950's and 1960's, before the social science community began questioning the wisdom of such marriages. Moreover, it is unclear that there is any net benefit to early marriage by pregnant teenagers. Granted, among a sample of black Baltimore teenagers studied prospectively by Furstenburg and colleagues for two decades, those who stayed married did fare better economically. But longstanding "shotgun" marriages were comparatively few, and those teens who divorced in short order actually fared worse than those who did not marry after becoming pregnant, so that the net effect of a (birth-legitimating) teenage marriage was nil.

Any further theoretical consideration of nonmarital fertility rates should be informed by trends in rates of *marital* fertility. Even with rises in the age at first marriage and a growing propensity to never marry, especially among blacks, the vast majority of women, both black and white, do spend some portion of their reproductive lives in wedlock. The large differences in nonmarital fertility rates between blacks and whites must be considered against the comparatively small fertility differences among married women and the growing black-white convergence in expected family size (*e.g.*, U.S. Bureau of the Census 1988). Current rates of nonmarital fertility appear so high in large part because marital fertility rates, among both blacks and whites, have been declining so much in the United States during the past three decades.

Nonmarital Fertility Ratios

This decline in marital fertility, coupled with a downward trend in nuptiality (operationalized as the proportion of women married by a given age), accounts for the trends shown in Figure 7. Nonmarital

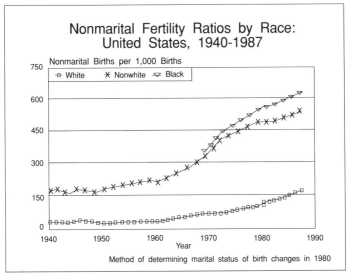

Figure 7. Nonmarital fertility ratios for both blacks and whites have risen precipitously. In 1987, three-in-five black children and one-in-six white children were born out-of-wedlock.

fertility *ratios* — the number of children born out of wedlock per 1,000 births — have increased steadily since 1940 among both whites and nonwhites, with most of the change having occurred since 1960. This is in spite of the fact that nonmarital fertility *rates* for blacks were far lower in the 1980's than they were in the 1960's. Had the marital fertility and marital status of blacks remained constant at 1963 levels, and only the age structure and rates of nonmarital fertility changed, then the nonmarital fertility ratio for blacks in 1983 would have been 205 — 20% lower than the ratio which obtained in 1963 and far below the actual 1983 ratio of 578. A similarly standardized ratio for whites as of 1983 would have been 45, versus the actual observed ratio of 125 (Smith and Cutright 1988).

Thus the fact that over 60% of all black children born in 1987 were out of wedlock is as much a commentary on declining nuptiality and marital fertility as it is a measure of the extent of nonmarital childbearing in the subpopulation. But measured from the standpoint of the child, the situation is acute. Each black child born

during the 1980's is more likely than not to be the offspring of a
nonmarried woman. Similar comments obtain with respect to
cohort-differentiated social roles later in the life cycle — *e.g.*, grades
of school children. The situation is less grave among whites, where
"only" one-in-six children is born out of wedlock. To put this in some
perspective, the chance that a white baby born in 1987 was
conceived and delivered out of wedlock is equivalent to the same
probability for a nonwhite baby born in the 1940's.

Why are these increases in the nonmarital fertility ratio so
important? As nonmarital fertility ratios go up, the marginal
distribution of nonmarital versus marital births shifts in the
direction of the former. This is important only insofar as life
chances are differentially conditioned on legitimacy status at birth.
In particular, most children born out of wedlock spend, by definition, at least some part of their life in a single-parent household.[7]
Girls living in such households are more likely to be sexually active,
to have premarital births of their own, to marry early and bear
children, and to have their own unions dissolve (Hogan and Kitagawa
1985; McLanahan and Bumpass 1988). These effects persist even
after controls for socioeconomic background and are not mitigated
by the subsequent introduction of stepparents (McLanahan and
Bumpass 1988). This suggests that the trends evinced in Figure 7
may be self-perpetuating.

Conversely, I have hypothesized elsewhere (Smith and Cutright
1988) that there is also a self-limiting aspect to these trends — that
as nonmarital childbearing becomes the norm rather than the
exception, differences in life chances between those born in and out
of wedlock may diminish. This is predicated on the assumption
that part of the handicap of a nonmarital birth is stigmatization.
However, the deleterious effects of living with a single parent are
just that — the effects of living with a single parent (generally
without a father), not the effects of being born out of wedlock *per se*.
Ironically, the situation of the many children born out of wedlock
may be ameliorated in *relative* terms as more and more children
born to married couples lose parents through divorce.

Trends in Divorce

Figure 8 displays total number of divorces (in thousands) for the
United States for the years 1950 to 1988.[8] During the 1950's, the
number of divorces held quite steady at around 380,000 per annum.

The number of divorces annually grew at an increasing rate into the early 1970's, and reached over a million in 1975. But by then the rate of increase was declining. The total number of divorces apparently peaked in 1981 — at over 1.2 million — and appears to have since reached a plateau. The net impression is of a logistic curve. This general impression still obtains after standardizing these totals for population size: Figure 9 gives divorce rates per 1,000 in the total population and over.

Figure 8. Both the number of divorces and the number of children involved in divorce rose steadily during the 1960s and '70s, but have levelled off in the 1980s.

Shadowing the growth in the number of annual divorces is the growth in the number of children involved in divorce. This curve is also shown in Figure 8 and has followed a *generally* similar pattern. There were approximately 300,000 children involved in divorces in 1950 and almost four times that many in 1979. When expressed as a rate — Figure 9 — child involvement in divorce tripled between the early 1950's and the early 1980's.

The intertwining of curves in Figure 8 for divorces and children involved in divorce is reflected in the bell-shaped pattern for average number of children per divorce decree, shown in Figure 10. In the early 1950's, each divorce involved on average only 0.8 children. As fertility rose during the 1950's, so too did the number of children per divorce decree. From 1964 to 1968 — a period approximately ten years after the peak of the Baby Boom — each divorce involved approximately 1.33 children. Since then, the number of children per decree has fallen steadily to just under one child per divorce in the 1980's. Just as the rise in this index coincided with a rise in fertility, so too has the decline coincided (at a lag) with sharp reductions in rates of marital childbearing.

This decline has also coincided with changes in the timing of fertility, especially first births (Rindfuss, Morgan, and Swicegood 1988). Divorce rates are highest at young ages and short marriage duration intervals. When childbearing is delayed within marriage,

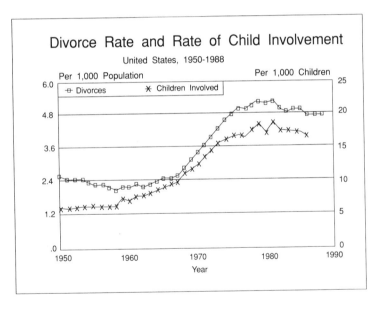

Figure 9. Both the divorce rate and the rate of child involvement in divorce peaked in the early 1980s.

Table 2. Period-specific divorce rates in the 1970's and 80's imply that approximately one-half of all new marriages in the U.S. will end in divorce.

Probabilities of Marital Dissolution
for Synthetic Marriage Cohorts
by Year

Year	Probability of Dissolution	Source
1973	44	Preston (1975)
1976-77	50	Weed (1980)
1980	57[a]	Martin and Bumpass (1989)
1982	51[a]	
1984	56[a]	
	(64)[a,b]	

Notes: [a]Includes separations, which may increase dissolution probability estimates by a factor of .05.

[b]Adjusted for underreporting.

there are — everything else being equal — fewer children involved in the average divorce (London 1989, pp. 2-3).[9]

Notwithstanding its depressant effect on marital satisfaction, the presence of children in marriage tends to diminish prospects for marital dissolution (see Morgan, Lye, and Condran [1988, pp. 111-113] and citations therein). However, there is at least suggestive evidence that the prophylactic effect of kids with respect to marriage may be on the wane (London 1989, p. 2). Also shown in Figure 10 is the average number of children per married couple household. In the 1950's and early 1960's, the average number of children in married couple households exceeded the average number of children in divorcing households by a substantial degree. But the gap narrowed during the 1960's and 70's, so that by the 1980's the two curves are indistinguishable: Married couple households have on average no more children than do divorcing couples.

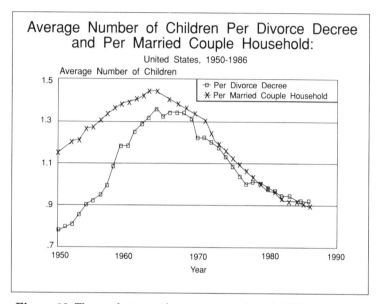

Figure 10. The gap between the average number of children per divorce decree and the average number of children per married couple household, which was substantial in the 1950s, has disappeared.

The convergence of these trends does need to be placed in proper context. Most studies regarding the effects of children on marital stability control for important factors related to divorce, such as age and duration of marriage. Even with the equivalence during the 1980's in the average number of children per divorce decree and the average number of children per married couple household, it may be that, all else equal, couples with children are less likely to divorce. For example, the average number of children per married couple household may be declining as the population ages and fewer married couples have children under age 18. Still, the data shown in Figure 10 do conform with attitudinal evidence of a declining belief that marriages should remain intact "for the sake of the children" (London 1989, p. 2), and it may be the case that the positive effect of children on marital stability is declining.[10]

Period-specific totals and rates of divorce are useful for conveying the flow of adults into divorce and children into single-parent households. However, they do not fully capture trends in prospects of divorce for at least two reasons. First, period-specific variability of divorce — fluctuations in annual rates of divorce — far exceed the variability of divorce as calculated for *marriage cohorts* (Preston and McDonald 1979). Long-term trends in rates of divorce — per existing marriage (Preston and McDonald 1979, p. 13) or per 1,000 population (Weed 1980, p. 2) — show "spikes" following World Wars I and II (the latter in particular) and a trough during the Great Depression, which have only minor effects on trends in divorce probabilities among marriage cohorts extant during the same period. "[T]he timing of divorce is more responsive to period-specific influences than is the volume of divorce that will be experienced by cohorts at risk during the period" (Preston and McDonald 1979, p. 12).

Second, period-specific measures of divorce can be highly dependent on the composition of the at-risk population, especially with respect to such factors as age at marriage and duration of marriage. Thus Martin and Bumpass (1989) argue that a 10% downturn in the crude divorce rate (divorces per 1,000 population) during the 1980's is not indicative of a declining propensity to divorce in the population. Instead, the high divorce rates of the late 1970's are attributed in part to the compositional effects of the Baby Boom. A disproportionate number of marriages contracted during the 1970's were to teenagers (Wilson 1985), and the proportion of short-duration marriages was unusually high as well. Because age at marriage and duration of marriage are both negatively correlated with likelihood of divorce, the "aging" of the population during the 1980's might well be expected to result in less aggregate divorce, without any changes in age at marriage- or duration-specific probabilities of marital dissolution.

One method of "correcting" for compositional differences over time in the distribution of marriages by duration is to calculate probabilities of marital dissolution for *synthetic marriage cohorts*. Marriages contracted in a given year are "survived" across duration-specific divorce probabilities obtaining in that year.[11] The result is a probability of divorce given exposure to prevailing duration-specific divorce rates. Some estimates of probabilities of marital dissolution for synthetic marriage cohorts are shown in Table 2 for selected years. The U.S. has almost definitely reached the point where over half of all marriages contracted annually will end in divorce. To the extent that Martin and Bumpass' (1989) adjustments for underreporting of divorce are correct, the total number of failed marriages per marriage cohort may be approaching two-thirds.

Statistics such as these are sometimes adduced to claim that 50% of existing marriages are likely to end in divorce. This is incorrect. The stock of existing marriages at any given point in time is *positively selected* with respect to durability. Marriages of long duration abound. Given prevailing duration-specific dissolution probabilities, Martin and Bumpass (1989, p. 40) calculate that only 21% of marriages intact as of June 1985 will eventually be dissolved.

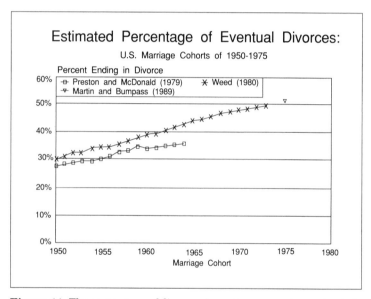

Figure 11. The percentage of divorces in post-war marriage cohorts has risen steadily, to approximately 50% for those contracted in the mid 1970s.

The chief criticism of divorce and/or dissolution probabilities for synthetic marriage cohorts is that they may exaggerate the experience of actual marriage cohorts. Just as no birth cohort of women had total fertility rates as high as those prevailing at the height of the Baby Boom, perhaps no marriage cohort will have a divorce experience as great as that obtaining cross-sectionally circa 1980.

Such might be the case, for example, if strong selection processes work within cohorts — if high rates of dissolution at short durations in a cohort mean low rates of divorce in the same cohort at older ages. Although such an argument is plausible, there is no evidence in its favor. Preston and McDonald (1979) calculated probabilities of divorce for cohorts of marriages contracted since the Civil War. For more recent cohorts, who had marriages still at risk of divorce, it was assumed that the necessary duration-specific divorce and mortality rates needed to "complete" their marriages were those observed as of 1969. The result is a surprisingly smooth exponential curve, beginning at 5% for the marriage cohort of 1867 and reaching 36% for the marriage cohort of 1964. Weed (1980) updated this series, using duration-specific divorce and mortality probabilities from 1976-77. See Figure 11. Some of the increase in probability of divorce relative to that estimated by Preston and McDonald (1979) is a result of the higher levels of divorce in 1976-77 than in 1969. But Weed (1980) was also able to observe the divorce experience of many of these cohorts over several more years when their incidence of divorce was in fact higher than that assumed based on the prevalence of 1969 rates. Weed's (1980) calculations show that actual marriage cohorts contracted during the early 1970's should indeed approach the 50% divorce rate predicted via the synthetic marriage cohort approach, and Martin and Bumpass (1989) provide an estimate of 51% for the marriage cohort of 1975. Nor is there any evidence that divorce has abated during the 1980's. Martin and Bumpass (1989, p. 39) report that the percentage of marriages ending within five years was 22% for those marrying in the late 1970's and 23% for those marrying in the early 1980's.

The recent analysis of Martin and Bumpass (1989) also affords us a look at recent trends in the *effects* of several important factors on the likelihood of divorce, separately for both whites and blacks. All effects are *ceteris paribus* — net of duration and other social factors.

Age at marriage: Among whites, teenage marriages are roughly twice as likely to be dissolved as those at other ages. This effect has held steady for marriages contracted between 1970 and 1985, even though the relative frequency of teenage marriage declined after the early 1970's (Wilson 1985). Among blacks, the age differential declined from the early 1970's to the early 1980's to the point where marriages contracted by teenagers appear no more likely than those contracted by older women to end in divorce or separation.[12]

Education: The negative relationship between women's education and marital disruption increased across marriage cohorts from the early 1970's to the early 1980's. For the first marriage cohorts of 1980-85, white women were twice as likely and black women two-and-one-half times as likely to divorce if they had less than twelve years of education than if they had more than twelve years. Ten years earlier, educational differences were negligible.

Children before marriage: There is no trend. Entering a first marriage with premarital offspring raises the odds of divorce by 70% among whites, but only 16% among blacks. "This difference by race may well reflect the more 'deviant' status of an unmarried mother among whites than among blacks. . . ." (Martin and Bumpass 1989, p. 43).

Discussion

To make sense of the trends described above, they must be placed in a larger context. I have already alluded to parallel demographic trends — changes in the timing of marriage, declines in fertility within marriage — but there are also larger social and economic trends which must be considered.

It is sometimes argued that the increase in divorce and the rise in nonmarital childbearing (never mind that the latter is unsubstantiated by our inspection of black nonmarital fertility rates) are indicators of a decline in "traditional" family values. The subtext is that if these values were more widely endorsed and adhered to by the society as a whole, both divorce and nonmarital childbearing would become less pervasive.

There is certainly ample evidence that American attitudes have changed during the period surveyed here, not only toward premarital sexual activity, marriage, and divorce, but also toward intrafamilial roles and the general place of women in the society (*e.g.*, Veroff, Douvan, and Kulka 1981; McLaughlin *et al.* 1988, pp. 168-191). It is also the case that attention to changing norms, attitudes, and values can provide a useful framework for understanding demographic trends (*e.g.*, Preston 1987). However, I would caution against too great an emphasis on values, attitudes, and norms as causative agents behind trends in nonmarital fertility and divorce for at least four reasons.

First, values may be vestigial. They may lag social change rather than lead it. This is exemplified by Davis' (1984) analysis of the decline in the "breadwinner/homemaker" family system in favor of an "egalitarian" family. Davis argues that the former arrangement, which we incorrectly label as "traditional," was in fact fairly short and transient in longer historical perspective, reflecting a fairly limited era in which industrialization led to the physical separation of work from home and acute specialization in sex roles for men and women. Maintenance of this system required, among other things, the inculcation of strong norms regarding the economic responsibility of men toward their wives and children, with strong attendant proscriptions against nonmarital sexual activity and childbearing, plus divorce. But, according to Davis (1984), the internal contradictions of the system — the dominant economic position of men coupled with their removal from the household — contained the seeds of its own destruction, and in practical social, economic, and demographic terms the breadwinner/homemaker system was coming apart long before its ideological heyday, the 1950's.

Second, changing attitudes and values may reflect changing demographic circumstances and not vice versa. According to Davis and van den Oever (1982, p. 508):

> [D]emographic changes . . . reduce the share of marriage
> and children in women's lives and, by doing so, lead women
> to attach less importance to their domestic role. Women's
> prospects are that around two-thirds of their adult years
> will be spent without children in the household and possi-
> bly half to two-thirds without a husband. For long periods
> they will probably be thrown on their own resources and
> will need employment. This means that, in planning their
> lives, they must look to their own careers as separate
> individuals. For best results, they must enter employment
> while young and remain employed consistently to build up
> experience, seniority, reputation, and whatever cumulative
> benefit comes from occupational commitment.

Thus begins a process in which marriage is increasingly devalued:

> Once under way, the system of change exhibits a dynamic
> of its own. Insofar as demographic trends lead women to
> downgrade marriage and stress employment, they also lead

them to reduce not only their dependence on their husbands, but also their service to them. Men, in turn, are
induced to reconsider the costs and benefits of marriage.
They sense that, at older ages, men are increasingly scarce
compared with women, that they do not have to marry to
enjoy female company, and that if they do marry, their role
as father and family head has somehow been eroded.

They go on to term the feminist movement

an inevitable response to basic demographic changes . . . an
ideological reaction to alterations in the underlying conditions of life. . . . The . . . extreme . . . goal of the feminist
movement, . . . the rejection of all division of labor based on
sex, . . . is understandable, because it extrapolates to its
end the actual diminution of marriage and childbearing in
women's lives. . . . (Davis and van den Oever 1982, pp. 508-
509).

Third, even where attitudes and values are logically antecedent
to behavior, the link may be weak. Thornton and Camburn (1987)
consider the influence of mothers' attitudes and behaviors regarding premarital sexual activity on the same attitudes and behaviors
of their teenage children (whites only). The mothers' attitudes and
behaviors did explain significant proportions of the attitudes and
behaviors of their children, but the effects were greater with
respect to their children's *attitudes* toward premarital sexual
activity than with respect to their children's actual *behavior*.

Fourth, "traditional" family ideologies may be dysfunctional
with respect to, in particular, premarital childbearing. Anderson's
(1989) ethnography of sex codes and family life among inner-city
black youth depicts an environment in which young girls enthusi-
astically embrace a family ideal more consonant with television
dreams than with the reality of their environment.

This dream involves having a boyfriend, a fiancé, a husband, and the fairy-tale prospect of living happily ever
after in a nice house in a neighborhood with one's children
— essentially the dream of the middle-class American
lifestyle, complete with the nuclear family. It is nurtured
by a daily involvement with afternoon television soap
operas, or "stories," as the women call them. The heroes or

> heroines of these stories may be white and middle-class, but for many, these characteristics only make them more attractive as role models. Many girls dream of the role of the comfortable middle-class housewife portrayed on television, even though they see that their peers can only approximate that role (Anderson 1989, p. 62).

The problem is that these dreams get used against them by boys who pay lip service to the same values in the pursuit of their adolescent goal — sexual conquest. This drama is not unique to poor black adolescents — something similar surely goes on among whites and those with higher incomes. The difference is that the economic and social environment is so poor that males have little to lose by behaving irresponsibly and few prospects for enacting the roles that the girls wish upon them, even if they were desirous of doing so.

There are also reasons to be cautious about identifying social and economic trends with the trends in nonmarital fertility and divorce described here. For example, increases in female labor force participation and the declining economic dependence of married women on their spouses (Sorensen and McLanahan 1987) may be adduced as explanations for the rising tide of divorce. But the threat of divorce may be as much cause as consequence, and the parallel movement in these series may reflect common structural conditions. These may include, as examples, fundamental tensions in the "traditional" marriage and family system (Davis 1984), problems with maintenance of a "family wage" (Vedder 1988), and black/white differences in the relative economic opportunities of men and women (Farley 1988).

— Herbert L. Smith is assistant professor of sociology and research associate at the Population Studies Center, University of Pennsylvania.

This is the revised text of a paper presented at the conference on "The Retreat from Marriage," sponsored by The Rockford Institute, Rockford, Illinois, 11-12 May 1989. My colleagues Phil Morgan and Sam Preston, plus the conference participants, provided helpful comments on the earlier draft of this paper. Kathy London and Barbara Wilson of the National Center for Health Statistics provided timely information regarding divorce statistics.

ENDNOTES

[1]*Remarriage following divorce is quite common. Schoen* et al. *(1985) estimate that approximately 80% of divorced men and 75% of divorced women subsequently remarry and that these remarriage probabilities have changed very little across the twentieth century, even as the proportion of men and women divorcing has increased. Second and higher-order marriages are, however, more prone to divorce than are first marriages (Wilson 1989). Cherlin's (1978) explanation is that remarriage is an "incomplete institution," lacking the institutionalized normative support, household organization, and family roles of first marriages.*

[2]*Martin and Bumpass (1989, fn10), citing McLanahan and Bumpass (1986), state that "[a]bout one-third of all nonmarital births . . . occur after marital disruption." But I find no evidence for this statistic in the latter source and evidence against it in the June 1987 Current Population Survey (U.S. Bureau of the Census 1988, Table 4), which reports that there were 583,000 (never married) women who had had a child in the previous twelve months, as against 126,000 women who were widowed or divorced. If we ignore multiple births and the few women having two births in the same twelve-month interval, then only 18% of births to unmarried women would be to women who had previously been married. But even this overstates the percentage of nonmarital births to ever-married, because some of the births to women who were widowed or divorced were conceived while the women were still married, in which case they are not officially considered to be nonmarital births (see the discussion of definitions of nonmarital fertility in the section following). If "marital disruption" is considered to include* separation *as operationalized by the Census marital status category "married, husband absent," then there were an additional 127,000 women with disrupted marriages who had a birth during the previous twelve months. Again, these would not be considered nonmarital births in the legal sense, but if we redefine nonmarital fertility as "fertility to women not living with a husband," then it can be said that 30% of nonmarital births occur to women who have been married, which may explain the statistic cited by Martin and Bumpass (1989, fn10). In fact, in earlier years this latter percentage was much higher, e.g., 48% in the twelve months prior to June 1976 (U.S. Bureau of the Census 1988, Table D).*

[3]*The "probability" interpretation of rates must be tempered by the recognition that (a) probabilities of an event in an interval are nonlinear functions of central rates obtaining in this interval, with the discrepancy between probabilities and rates (probabilities are always lower) increasing as rates increase; and (b) rates are relative to mid-year populations that have been selectively reduced relative to the population at the start of the year by the exit of women who marry, with some of these marriages due to premarital pregnancies.*

[4]*These rates are for single years from 1960 through 1987. Prior to 1960, trends are based on data for 1940, 1950, and 1955 only, so that there is no possibility of picking up short-term fluctuations during this earlier period. This stipulation obtains for all other figures in this subsection, save for Figure 3, which is based on single-year data.*

[5]*Readers should be aware that Figures 4 through 6 use different vertical (rate) scales. Because the maximum level of white rates is so much lower than that for either nonwhites or blacks, the vertical scale for whites is more detailed. Shifts of five births*

per thousand appear large in Figure 4 for whites, but insignificant in Figures 5 and 6 for nonwhites and blacks. Thus all comments about "volatility," "constancy," etc. are specific to subpopulations.

[6]*The caution in this statement stems from the recognition that changes made in 1980 in the measurement of nonmarital childbearing appear to have significantly increased white fertility rates to such an extent that comparison of pre- and post-1980 trends is temporarily vitiated. See Figure 4.*

[7]*The exception would be those children legally born out of wedlock to couples who are cohabiting. Such unions are, however, far more likely to break up than marital unions.*

[8]*All data in Figures 8 through 10 for years through 1984 are from London (1989), except in Figure 10, for the average number of children per married couple household for 1950 and 1952-1955, which are from various Household Characteristics issues of the P-20 Series of the U.S. Bureau of the Census' Current Population Reports. Data from subsequent years are from various Monthly Vital Statistics Reports of the National Center for Health Statistics and from the P-20 and P-25 Series of the Current Population Reports.*

[9]*An alternative or adjunct explanation for the recent decline in number of children per divorce decree resides in the changing composition of the divorcing population. In particular, second and higher-order marriages are far less likely than first marriages to involve children (e.g., Wilson 1989, p. 17, Table S). However, there has been no marked shift in the composition of divorces toward those involving second or higher-order marriages. I have calculated, based on the method of indirect standardization, that changes in the relative frequency of second and higher-divorces are responsible for only the most minor of declines since the late 1960's (of perhaps .01 children) in the average number of children per decree.*

[10]*Variations in populations studied, sample definitions, controls, and methods of analysis make it difficult to put together a consistent series of such effects across studies.*

[11]*Allowance is also made for existing mortality risks, since mortality "competes" with divorce as a means of terminating marriages.*

[12]*This is based on Table 2 of Martin and Bumpass (1989). The accompanying text (p. 42) is in error (L. Bumpass, personal communication).*

REFERENCES

Anderson, Elijah. 1989. "Sex Codes and Family Life Among Poor Inner-City Youth." The Annals of the American Academy of Political and Social Science **501**:59-78.

Cherlin, Andrew. 1978. "Remarriage as an Incomplete Institution." American Journal of Sociology **84**:634-650.

Cutright, Phillips. 1971. "Illegitimacy: Myths, Causes, and Cures." Family Planning Perspectives **3**:25-48.

Cutright, Phillips, and Herbert L. Smith. 1986. "Trends in Illegitimacy Among Five English-Speaking Populations." Demography **23**:563-578.

——. *1988. "Intermediate Determinants of Racial Differences in 1980 U.S. Nonmarital Fertility Rates."* Family Planning Perspectives **20**:119-123.

Davis, Kingsley. 1984. "Wives and Work: Consequences of the Sex Role Revolution." Population and Development Review **10**:397-417.

Davis, Kingsley, and Piotrenella van den Oever. 1982. "Demographic Foundations of New Sex Roles." Population and Development Review 8:495-511.

Easterlin, Richard A. 1980. Birth and Fortune: The Impact of Numbers on Personal Welfare. New York: Basic.

Espenshade, Thomas J. 1985. "Marriage Trends in America: Estimates, Implications, and Underlying Causes." Population and Development Review 11:193-246.

Farley, Reynolds. 1988. "After the Starting Line: Blacks and Women in an Uphill Race." Demography 25:477-495.

Henshaw, Stanley K. 1987. "Characteristics of U.S. Women Having Abortions, 1982-1983." Family Planning Perspectives 19:5-9.

Hofferth, Sandra L., and Cheryl D. Hayes (eds.). 1987. Risking the Future: Adolescent Sexuality, Pregnancy, and Childbearing. Washington, D.C.: National Academy Press.

Hofferth, Sandra L., Joan R. Kahn, and Wendy Baldwin. 1987. "Premarital Sexual Activity Among U.S. Teenage Women Over the Past Three Decades." Family Planning Perspectives 19:46-53.

Hogan, Dennis P., and Evelyn M. Kitagawa. 1985. "The Impact of Social Status, Family Structure, and Neighborhood on the Fertility of Black Adolescents." American Journal of Sociology 90:825-855.

Jones, Jo Ann, Joan R. Kahn, Allan Parnell, Ronald R. Rindfuss, and C. Gray Swicegood. 1985. "Nonmarital Childbearing: Divergent Legal and Social Concerns." Population and Development Review 11:677-693.

Lieberson, Stanley, and Mary C. Waters. 1988. From Many Strands: Ethnic and Racial Groups in Contemporary America. New York: Russell Sage Foundation.

London, Kathryn A. 1989. Children of Divorce. Vital and Health Statistics, Series 21, No. 46. DHHS Pub. No. (PHS) 89-1924. Washington, D.C.: U.S. Government Printing Office.

Martin, Teresa Castro, and Larry L. Bumpass. 1989. "Recent Trends in Marital Disruption." Demography 26:37-51.

McLanahan, Sara, and Larry L. Bumpass. 1988. "Intergenerational Consequences of Family Disruption." American Journal of Sociology 94:130-152.

McLaughlin, Steven D., Barbara D. Melber, John O.G. Billy, Denise M. Zimmerle, Linda D. Winges, and Terry R. Johnson. 1988. The Changing Lives of American Women. Chapel Hill, N.C.: The University of North Carolina Press.

Morgan, S. Philip, Diane N. Lye, and Gretchen A. Condran. 1988. "Sons, Daughters, and the Risk of Marital Disruption." American Journal of Sociology 94:110-129.

Nathanson, Constance A., and Young J. Kim. 1989. "Components of Change in Adolescent Fertility, 1971-1979." Demography 26:85-98.

National Center for Health Statistics. 1988a. Vital Statistics of the United States, 1984, Vol. III, Marriage and Divorce. DHHS Pub. No. (PHS) 88-1103. Washington, D.C.: U.S. Government Printing Office.

———. 1988b. Vital Statistics of the United States, 1986, Vol. I., Natality. DHHS Pub. No. (PHS) 88-1123. Washington, D.C.: U.S. Government Printing Office.

———. 1989. "Annual Summary of Births, Marriages, Divorces, and Deaths: United States, 1988." Monthly Vital Statistics Reports, Vol. 37, No. 13. Washington, D.C.: U.S. Government Printing Office.

Preston, Samuel H. 1975. "Estimating the Proportion of American Marriages That End in Divorce." Sociological Methods and Research 3:435-460.

——. 1987. *"Changing Values and Falling Birth Rates."* Pp. 176-195 in Below-Replacement Fertility in Industrial Societies: Causes, Consequences, Policies *(Supplement to* Population and Development Review *12), edited by Kingsley Davis, Mikhail S. Bernstam, and Rita Ricardo-Campbell. New York: The Population Council.*

Preston, Samuel H., and John McDonald. 1979. *"The Incidence of Divorce within Cohorts of American Marriages Contracted Since the Civil War."* Demography **16**:1-26.

Rindfuss, Ronald R., S. Philip Morgan, and Gray Swicegood. 1988. First Births in America: Changes in the Timing of Parenthood. *Berkeley and Los Angeles: University of California Press.*

Schoen, Robert, William Urton, Karen Woodrow, and John Baj. 1985. *"Marriage and Divorce in Twentieth-Century American Cohorts."* Demography **22**:101-114.

Smith, Herbert L., and Phillips Cutright. 1988. *"Thinking About Change in Illegitimacy Ratios: United States, 1963-1983."* Demography **25**:235-247.

Sorensen, Annemette, and Sara McLanahan. 1987. *"Married Women's Economic Dependency, 1940-1980."* American Journal of Sociology **93**:659-687.

Tanfer, Koray, and Marjorie C. Horn. 1985. *"Contraceptive Use, Pregnancy and Fertility Patterns Among Single American Women in Their Twenties."* Family Planning Perspectives **17**:10-18.

Thornton, Arland, and Donald Camburn. 1987. *"The Influence of the Family on Premarital Sexual Attitudes and Behavior."* Demography **24**:323-340.

U.S. Bureau of the Census. 1988. Fertility of American Women: June 1987, *Current Population Reports, Series P-20, No. 247. Washington, D.C.: U.S. Government Printing Office.*

——. 1989. Statistical Abstract of the United States: 1989 *(109th edition). Washington, D.C.: U.S. Government Printing Office.*

Vedder, Richard. 1988. *"The Destruction and Reconstruction of the Family Wage in the United States, 1960-2000."* Pp. 79-100 in The Family Wage: Work, Gender, and Children in the Modern Economy, *edited by Bryce J. Christensen. Rockford, Ill.: The Rockford Institute.*

Veroff, Joseph, Elizabeth Douvan, and Richard A. Kulka. 1981. The Inner American: A Self-Portrait from 1957 to 1976. *New York: Basic Books.*

Vinovskis, Maris A. 1988. An "Epidemic" of Adolescent Pregnancy? Some Historical and Policy Considerations. *New York: Oxford University Press.*

Vinovskis, Maris A. P., and Lindsay Chase-Lansdale. 1987. *"Should We Discourage Teenage Marriage?"* Public Interest **87**:23-37.

Weed, James A. 1980. National Estimates of Marriage Dissolution and Survivorship. *Vital and Health Statistics, Series 3, No. 19 IV. DHHS Pub. No. (PHS) 81-1403. Washington, D.C.: U.S. Government Printing Office.*

Wilson, Barbara Foley. 1985. Teenage Marriage and Divorce, United States, 1970-81. *Vital and Health Statistics, Series 21, No. 43. DHHS Pub. No. (PHS) 85-1921. Washington, D.C.: U.S. Government Printing Office.*

——. 1989. Remarriages and Subsequent Divorces: United States. *Vital and Health Statistics, Series 21, No. 45. DHHS Pub. No. (PHS) 89-1923. Washington, D.C.: U.S. Government Printing Office.*

Zelnik, Melvin, and John F. Kantner. 1980. *"Sexual Activity, Contraceptive Use and Pregnancy among Metropolitan-Area Teenagers: 1971-1979."* Family Planning Perspectives **12**:230-237.

The Social and Cultural Meaning of Contemporary Marriage

by Norval Glenn

In one sense there has been an unmistakable retreat from marriage in the United States in recent years. The percentage of persons married has declined at all adult age levels, and people are on the average spending a substantially smaller proportion of their lives married than they did in the recent past. However, beyond these clear changes, the extent to which there has been a retreat from marriage is controversial. The views range from the belief that deinstitutionalization of marriage is occurring to the position that the institution of marriage is just as strong and healthy as it ever has been.

Proponents of the former view support it by citing the steep increase in divorce in the decade following 1965 and the continuing instability of marriages, increased nonmarital cohabitation, the fact that almost a fourth of all births in recent years have been out of wedlock, and changes in family law whereby divorce by mutual consent of the spouses has become available in all 50 states, and divorce by the unilateral choice of either spouse is in practice available in almost all, if not all, of the states. According to this view, the behavior of individuals and the actions of legislatures indicate a weakening of the values that undergird the institution of marriage.

At least until recently, a more common view among family social scientists was that recent changes in marriage are adaptive rather than indicative of decline or disintegration. Supporters of this view claim that divorce almost always reflects the rejection of a particular marriage and not the institution of marriage, that divorce and remarriage are means whereby poor marriages are replaced by better ones and the marital institution is kept viable, and that nonmarital cohabitation in the United States is generally a prelude to marriage rather than a substitute for it. This view, which John Scanzoni has labelled the "progressive" one,[1] includes the belief that contemporary marriages, unstable though they are, generally serve the needs of American adults at least as well as did the more stable marriages of the recent past.

There are, of course, intermediate positions between these extremes, including the view that there are still individual and societal needs that only marriage can serve, but which at least temporarily it is not serving well.

My purpose here is to present and discuss some evidence relating to the question of what is happening to American marriage. I do not try to cover all of the evidence that could be brought to bear on the question nor do I pretend to give a definitive answer to it. Rather, I restrict myself to some national survey data about how Americans feel about their marriages and how well, relative to the recent past, marriage is now serving the needs of adults. The issue of how well marriage is serving individuals' needs concerns causation, and only tentative causal inferences can be made on the basis of survey data. Indeed, contrary to the apparent beliefs of many social scientists, survey data are inherently limited in their ability to provide insight and understanding. Nevertheless, the data I present and discuss here are an important part of the total corpus of evidence that can help us to understand the social and cultural meaning of recent changes in American marriage.

My decision to focus on how well marriage is serving the needs of adult individuals reflects the fact that American marriage is, and long has been, what I call "hedonistic" for the lack of a better adjective.[2] Hedonistic marriage, which has been rare historically, exists largely to serve the needs and desires of married individuals, according to the prevailing values in the society. In American society, as in almost any other one, many people when asked the purpose of marriage will say "to have children," or something to that effect, but in response to a question about the reason for having children will say that it is to provide pleasure and gratification to the parents. Thus the ultimate end of marriage is to provide satisfaction to the parents and having children is only a means to that end, at least in the minds of most persons who are married or contemplating marriage. In contrast, a more common explicit purpose of marriage historically has been to have children for the sake of the kinship group, society, or Deity. When Americans talk about the success of marriages, they tend to use such terms as happiness and satisfaction. Family social scientists and psychologists likewise tend to define marital success in terms of happiness and satisfaction and such similar concepts as marital adjustment. I know of no American study of "marital success" that has defined success in terms of how well the marriages serve the needs of extended families, communities, the entire society, or even children.

What I call hedonistic marriage is of course associated with the conjugal family system in which the basic family unit is the nuclear one — consisting of husband, wife, and any offspring living with them — rather than the extended family or larger kinship group. Marriage now tends to be highly hedonistic throughout the Western world and is becoming at least moderately so in many non-Western societies. However, marriage is more hedonistic in the United States than in most other contemporary societies, and it seems to me that American marriage has become increasingly hedonistic in recent decades.

Given Americans' highly hedonistic orientation toward marriage, their motivation to marry and their commitment to the institution of marriage must be affected by their perception of how well marriage is serving the needs and desires of married persons. And this perception in turn should be affected by how well marriage is in fact serving the hedonistic goals of adults. Therefore, an assessment of the consequences of marriage on the happiness and satisfaction of adults is necessary (though not sufficient) for an understanding of any social and cultural retreat from, or deinstitutionalization of, marriage.

Trends in Reported Marital Happiness

Hundreds of studies conducted in recent years have dealt with how Americans feel about their marriages, and many of the studies have used scales consisting of several questions to measure the feelings. However, most of the studies have used unrepresentative samples of married persons and have not gauged feelings about marriages in ways strictly comparable to those used in other studies. The only available data suitable for studying year-by-year changes in the total society in how people feel about their marriages are responses to the simple question "Taking things all together, how would you describe your marriage? Would you say that your marriage is very happy, pretty happy, or not too happy?"[3]

Just how the responses to this question should be interpreted is debatable. Since almost two-thirds of the persons who have re-

sponded to the question in recent years have chosen "very happy,"
a possible interpretation is that most married Americans feel very
positively about their marriages. However, there are reasons to
believe that there is considerable overreporting of marital happiness, both because people may be reluctant to admit to an inter-
viewer that they feel less than very positively about their marriages and because some people are likely to be reluctant to admit
negative feelings about their marriages even to themselves. A good
many of the persons who say that their marriages are "very happy"
will report negative feelings in response to more specific questions,
and those who report that their marriages are less than very happy
seem almost always to have some fairly serious marital problems.[4]

TABLE 1
Percentage of married persons who reported that their mar-
riages were "very happy," by sex and period, United States
national samples

Pooled data from surveys conducted in:	Males (N)	Females (N)
1973, 1974, 1975, 1976, & 1977	70 (2,408)	66 (2,656)
1978, 1980, 1982, & 1983	67 (1,734)	64 (1,909)
1984, 1985, 1986, 1987, & 1988	64 (1,917)	62 (2,169)
Change	-6	-4

*Source: Computed from data from the General Social Surveys conducted
by the National Opinion Research Center. Data are for persons age 18 and
older.*

How recent changes in reported marital happiness should be interpreted is also debatable. The trend has been distinctly downward (see Table 1), but since the change has not been very large, a possible interpretation is that no substantial deterioration in the quality of American marriages has occurred. However, even a stable level of reported marital happiness is inconsistent with the most optimistic views of recent trends in American marriage. It has become almost standard practice among marriage-and-the-family and family textbook writers to point out that the steep increase in divorce since around 1965 does not indicate that there has been a corresponding deterioration in marital success (defined, as always, in hedonistic terms). Rather, it is argued, persons may simply have become less willing to tolerate unsatisfactory marriages. According to this view, an increased willingness to divorce to end poor marriages may indicate that having a good marriage is now more important to people than ever before.

If this argument is correct, the feelings toward their marriages of persons in intact marriages should be more positive now, on the average, than they were before the divorce rate went up. Unsatisfactory marriages should now be more readily terminated, and thus there should be fewer of them in the population of marriages at any given time to bring down the average level of reported marital happiness. However, the level of reported marital happiness declined moderately rather than increased from the early-to-middle 1970's to the middle-to-late 1980's (Table 1)[5] — a time during which the propensity to divorce increased.[6]

Andrew Greeley has argued that the decrease in reported marital happiness shown in Table 1 resulted only from an increase in the average age of married persons, since at each age level little or no decrease occurred.[7] However, there is no reason to think that age in itself has any effect on how people evaluate their marriages; rather, it seems likely that older persons tend to evaluate their marriages less positively than younger ones only because the former have been married longer on the average.[8] Indeed, when duration of marriage is statistically held constant, age bears virtually no relationship to reported marital happiness. Therefore, it is important that the decline in reported marital happiness occurred at almost all durations of marriage in the case of persons in their first marriages (Table 2).[9]

TABLE 2
Percentage of persons in intact first marriages who reported that their marriages were "very happy," by period and duration of marriage, United States national samples

Duration of marriage (in years)	Pooled data from surveys conducted in:			Change
	1973, 1974, 1975, 1976, & 1977 (N)	1978, 1980, 1982, & 1983 (N)	1984, 1985, 1986, 1987, & 1988 (N)	
0-2	81 (231)	76 (169)	74 (219)	-7
3-5	68 (436)	66 (344)	62 (304)	-6
6-8	67 (380)	59 (265)	60 (282)	-7
9-11	63 (309)	67 (225)	54 (241)	-9
12-14	70 (312)	65 (217)	58 (228)	-12
15-19	61 (438)	59 (293)	62 (377)	+1
20-24	64 (421)	57 (224)	60 (291)	-4
25-29	69 (413)	67 (245)	61 (238)	-7
30-39	70 (752)	71 (565)	63 (508)	-7
40+	71 (626)	71 (474)	69 (636)	-2
Total	68 (4,318)	66 (3,021)	64 (2,830)	-4

Source: Computed from data from the General Social Surveys conducted by the National Opinion Research Center. Data are for persons age 18 and older.

The clearest evidence of a decline in marital success emerges when data on marital happiness are combined with data on separation and divorce. In Table 3, I report for three recent periods of time the percentages of ever-married, nonwidowed persons who were still in their first marriages and who reported that those marriages were "very happy" at different lengths of time after the marriages began.[10] All of the percentages are smaller for the latest than for the earliest period, and several of the decreases approach 15 percentage points.[11] Of the persons who first married in the early-to-middle 1970's, only a third were still married and said that their marriages were "very happy" by the middle-to-late 1980's. Since there was probably considerable overreporting of marital happiness, the real proportion of those marriages that were successful, as success is defined here, may well have been under a fourth.

TABLE 3
Percentage of ever-married, nonwidowed persons who
were in their first marriages and who reported that their
marriages were "very happy," by period and years since
first marriage, United States national samples

Pooled data from surveys conducted in:

Years since 1st marriage	1973, 1974, 1975, 1976, & 1977 (N)	1978, 1980, 1982, & 1983 (N)	1984, 1985, 1986, 1987, & 1988 (N)	Change
0-2	77 (243)	71 (181)	68 (237)	-9
3-5	58 (506)	55 (414)	50 (375)	-8
6-8	54 (471)	44 (356)	45 (373)	- 9
9-11	46 (423)	45 (339)	33 (393)	-13
12-14	46 (425)	42 (330)	32 (415)	-14
15-19	42 (637)	35 (492)	34 (685)	- 8
20-24	47 (573)	34 (376)	33 (538)	-14
25-29	47 (605)	38 (437)	33 (438)	-14
30-39	53 (997)	49 (810)	40 (795)	-13
40+	54 (826)	50 (674)	48 (905)	-6
Total	52 (5,706)	45 (4,409)	41 (5,144)	-11

Source: Computed from data from the General Social Surveys conducted by the National Opinion Research Center. Data are for persons age 18 and older.

It is also clear from the data in Table 3 that the long-term rate of marital success of persons who married in the past 30 years or so will be much lower than that of persons who married earlier. Some of the difference in the percentages between persons in the middle and later durations of marriage may reflect a moderate average increase in marital happiness in the later durations (apparently associated with the children's leaving home, in the case of wives).[12] However, most of the difference reflects the fact that a larger percentage of the persons who first married ten to 30 years before the surveys were conducted than of those who married earlier had already separated or divorced.

The one favorable indication in the data in Table 3 is that more change occurred from the earliest to the middle period than from the middle to the latest one. This slowing of the change resulted solely from the leveling off of the divorce rate in the 1980's, since the decline in reported marital happiness was as great from the middle to the latest period as from the earliest to the middle one (Tables 1 and 2).

In brief, considering the trend in reported marital happiness in conjunction with the trend in separation and divorce leads to a less sanguine view of what is happening to American marriage than does a superficial examination of the marital happiness data by themselves. The data presented here are strong evidence for a decline in marital success unless reports of marital happiness are completely invalid, which is unlikely, or unless during the period covered persons became much less likely to overreport their marital happiness. The latter possibility should not be summarily dismissed, and I return to it below after I report some evidence that relates to it.

Trends in the Reported Global Happiness of Married Persons

People marry in hope of having a happy marriage and also in hope that the marriage will help to make their life in general happy. And, indeed, there is considerable evidence that marriage has often provided what people seek from it. Numerous studies have shown that on the average the reported personal (global) happiness of married persons is considerably higher than that of those who have never married, are separated or divorced, or are widowed. Such a finding cannot prove that marriage generally contributes to happiness, since happy people may be more inclined to marry and to stay married than less happy ones, but there are strong reasons to believe that marriage primarily affects happiness rather than vice versa.[13]

However, if marriage has contributed substantially to personal happiness, that effect seems to have weakened in recent years. At least the difference in reported happiness between married and never-married persons has decreased measurably in the United States, as shown by responses on national surveys to the question "Taken all together, how would you say things are these days — would you say that you are very happy, pretty happy, or not too happy?" The percentages of "very happy" responses of never-married and married persons ages 25-39 to very recent surveys and to those conducted during two earlier periods are shown in Table 4.[14] Since the early-to-middle 1970's, the difference between never-married and married persons has declined by more than half for

TABLE 4
Percentage of persons ages 25-39 who reported that they were "very happy," by marital status, sex, and period, United States national samples

Pooled data from surveys conducted in:	Never-Married (N)	Married (N)	Difference
MALES			
1972, 1973, 1974, 1975, & 1976	13 (159)	34 (812)	+21
1977, 1978, 1980, 1982, & 1983	21 (235)	32 (794)	+11
1984, 1985, 1986, 1987, & 1988	24 (319)	34 (678)	+10
Change	+11	0	-11
FEMALES			
1972, 1973, 1974, 1975, & 1976	14 (102)	43 (1,015)	+29
1977, 1978, 1980, 1982, & 1983	26 (219)	40 (942)	+14
1984, 1985, 1986, 1987, & 1988	22 (255)	38 (887)	+16
Change	+8	-5	-13

Source: Computed from data from the General Social Surveys conducted by the National Opinion Research Center.

males and by almost half for females. For males the change came about solely because the reported happiness of never-married persons increased, but for females it resulted from both an increase in the reported happiness of never-married persons and a decrease in that of married ones.

The reasons for the decline in the relationship between being married and reporting oneself to be very happy are far from clear, but since it has resulted in large measure from an increase in the reported happiness of never-married persons, the change could not be just a result of a decrease in marital happiness. One might speculate that in the 25-39 age range, a larger percentage of the never-married individuals now have fairly stable heterosexual relationships, including but not limited to cohabitation, that provide some of the emotional benefits of marriage.

Equally important for the purpose of assessing what is happening to American marriage is the moderate but important degree of indicated decline in the happiness of married young adult women. Until recently, young married women had, by a rather large margin, the highest average reported happiness of any category of the American population, whereas now their reported happiness is only moderately higher than that of some other categories, including young married men.[15]

Since virtually all of the indicated change in the relationship between marital status and reported happiness came between the earliest and the middle surveys drawn upon for the data in Table 4, it would seem that there was rapid change in the 1970's and very early 1980's followed by stability since then. However, the way in which data from different years were combined for Table 4 conceals the somewhat more complex pattern of change revealed by the three-year running averages in Table 5.[16] The difference between never-married and married persons declined almost steadily from the early 1970's through the middle 1980's, but then it increased rather sharply in the late 1980's. Since the data are from rather small samples and thus are subject to considerable random sampling error, it is too early to know whether or not the apparent reversal in the downward trend is real. And if the reversal is real, we cannot yet tell whether or not there will be a return to the strong relationship between marital status and reported happiness that existed in the early 1970's.

TABLE 5
Difference, in percentage points, between married and never-married persons ages 25-39 in "very happy" responses,* by sex, three-year running averages, 1972-1974 through 1986-1988, United States national samples

Years	Males	Females
1972, 1973, 1974	23	37
1973, 1974, 1975	22	32
1974, 1975, 1976	21	24
1975, 1976, 1977	18	20
1976, 1977, 1978	18	18
1977, 1978, 1980**	13	17
1978, 1980, 1982**	11	14
1980, 1982, 1983**	8	14
1982, 1983, 1984	9	16
1983, 1984, 1985	5	12
1984, 1985, 1986	4	13
1985, 1986, 1987	7	12
1986, 1987, 1988	14	17

Source: Computed from data from the General Research Social Surveys conducted by the National Opinion Research Center.

*The percentage of "very happy" responses was higher for married than for never-married persons at all dates for both males and females.

**No survey was conducted in 1979 or 1981.

In spite of the evidence for an upturn in the late 1980's in the strength of the relationship of marital status to reported happiness, the overall trend in the relationship is consistent with the downward trend in reported marital happiness. That is, the same underlying forces could account for both, and both trends are evidence that all is not well with the institution of marriage in this country. The consistency of the two trends makes it seem unlikely that the decline in reported marital happiness reflects merely a lessened tendency for persons to overreport their marital happiness.

The reported happiness of the separated and divorced is now well below that of either never-married or married persons, and its level did not change appreciably during the period covered by this study.[17] Therefore, the increase since the early 1970's in the

---

TABLE 6
Percentage of persons who reported that they were "very happy," by sex and period, United States national samples

Pooled data from surveys conducted in:	Males (N)	Females (N)
AGE 18 & OLDER		
1972, 1973, 1974, 1975, & 1976	32 (3,528)	36 (4,042)
1977, 1978, 1980, 1982, & 1983	32 (3,281)	35 (4,303)
1984, 1985, 1986, 1987, & 1988	32 (3,148)	33 (4,179)
Change	0	-3
AGES 25-39		
1972, 1973, 1974, 1975, & 1976	29 (1,047)	37 (1,288)
1977, 1978, 1980, 1982, & 1983	29 (1,162)	34 (1,455)
1984, 1985, 1986, 1987, & 1988	29 (1,136)	30 (1,462)
Change	+0	-7

Source: Computed from data from the General Social Surveys conducted by the National Opinion Research Center.

proportion of adults separated or divorced has tended to lower the level of reported happiness in the adult population as a whole. However, among men the increase in the reported happiness of never-married persons offset the effect of the increase in the proportion of persons separated or divorced, leaving the overall level of reported happiness the same in the middle-to-late 1980's as it was in the early-to-middle 1970's (Table 6). In contrast, the increase in the proportion of women who were separated or divorced combined with the decrease in reported happiness of married women to more than offset the increase in the reported happiness of never-married women, the result being a decline in the "very happy" percentages of three points in the total adult population and seven points among women ages 25-39 (Table 6).[18]

As I point out above, all causal conclusions based on data such as these must be tentative, but it appears that recent changes in marital status and in the effect of marital status on happiness have led to a distinct decline in the happiness of women, but have had no net effect on the happiness of men as a whole.

Trends in the Relationship of Marital Happiness to Global Happiness

Several studies have shown that reported marital and global happiness are closely related to one another.[19] That is, persons who report high marital happiness tend to report high global happiness and vice versa. There is more than one possible reason for this strong relationship, but the most likely one is that having a good marriage contributes to one's overall happiness. One might speculate that marriage has recently become less important to individuals in the United States, so that the quality of their marriages has come to bear a weaker relationship to their overall happiness or psychological well-being. For instance, as more women have careers, the quality of work life might become more important, and marriage less important, in determining women's happiness.

However, the relationship between reported marital and global happiness did not change measurably from the early-to-middle 1970's to the middle-to-late 1980's (Table 7). Furthermore, the level of reported happiness of persons who reported "very happy" marriages did not change to any important extent. At all three periods for which data are shown in Table 7, having a very happy marriage seems to have been virtually necessary for a high level of personal happiness of married persons, both men and women. On the other hand, having a very happy marriage seems not to have been sufficient for a high level of global happiness, although it seems to have been more nearly so for women than for men.[20] At all three periods, the relationship between the two kinds of reported happiness was appreciably stronger for women than for men.[21] In spite of increased involvement of married women in nonfamily activities, having a good marriage seems still to be more important to women than to men, and there is no evidence of a recent change in that difference.

If reports of marital happiness had become more nearly accurate

---

TABLE 7
Percentage of married persons who reported that they were "very happy," by level of reported marital happiness, sex, and period, United States national samples

Pooled data from surveys conducted in:	Marital happiness	Males (N)	Females (N)	Male-female difference
1973, 1974, 1975, 1976, & 1977	Very happy	52 (1,669)	63 (1,739)	
	Less than very happy	11 (735)	10 (917)	
	Difference	41	53	-12
1978, 1980, 1982, & 1983	Very happy	50 (1,218)	60 (1,218)	
	Less than very happy	10 (575)	8 (687)	
	Difference	40	52	-12
1984, 1985, 1986, 1987, & 1988	Very happy	54 (1,215)	62 (1,328)	
	Less than very happy	11 (690)	9 (830)	
	Difference	43	53	-10

Source: Computed from data from the General Social Surveys conducted by the National Opinion Research Center. Data are for persons age 18 and older.

during the period covered by this study (as I mention as a possibility above), everything else being equal, the relationship between reported marital and global happiness would have become stronger during the time covered by the data, and the global happiness of persons who reported "very happy" marriages would have increased. The absence of these changes is further evidence that the decrease in reported marital happiness shown in Tables 1 and 2 reflects a real change in how people felt about their marriages.

The data in Table 8 allow a comparison of the levels of reported

---

TABLE 8
Percentage of persons who reported that they were "very happy," by sex, marital status, and quality of marriage, pooled data from United States national surveys conducted in 1984, 1985, 1986, 1987, and 1988

	Males (N)	Females (N)
Married, very happy marriage	54 (1,215)	62 (1,218)
Married, less than very happy marriage	11 (690)	9 (830)
Widowed	24 (123)	29 (675)
Separated or divorced	17 (370)	19 (712)
Never-married	23 (741)	23 (629)

Source: Computed from data from the General Social Surveys conducted by the National Opinion Research Center. Data are for persons age 18 and older.

---

happiness of persons in marriages of high and low quality (according to self-reports) and in different unmarried statuses. The highest level of reported happiness, by a large margin, is for persons in marriages of high quality, but the lowest is for those in marriages of low quality.[22] In other words, from the standpoint of the individual, a poor marriage is not better than no marriage at all.[23] Most people probably have no precise knowledge of this pattern of happiness, but many are likely to be at least vaguely aware of it, and to the extent that it is perceived, it is likely to be highly conducive to marital instability. In view of the fact that prevailing values in this society encourage people to make decisions about marriage and divorce on the basis of hedonistic self-interest rather than duty or obligation, persons in marriages of low quality are likely to be highly motivated to try, through divorce and remarriage, to replace those marriages with ones of high quality. And persons in low quality marriages are likely to be fairly highly motivated to divorce even if they perceive that their chances for remarriage are low.

Interpretation of the Observed Trends

The evidence reviewed here is clearly not consistent with the most sanguine views of the state of American marriage. American women apparently are not as happy as they were a few years ago, and changes in the quality of marriages and in the percentage of women married seem to be largely responsible for the decline. American men, as a whole, seem not to have experienced any decline in happiness, but marriage appears to be contributing less to their psychological well-being than it once did.

On the other hand, the data I present are also not consistent with the more extreme views about a declining importance of marriage in American society. The psychological rewards of having a good marriage seem not to have declined appreciably, if at all, even though attaining such a marriage has apparently become more difficult. It is likely, therefore, that having a good marriage is still an important goal of most Americans.[24]

By itself, the evidence presented and discussed here can provide only a partial and sketchy view of what is happening to American marriage. However, the tentative picture it provides is of a crucially important institution that is not serving the psychological needs of American adults especially well. There is little indication that large numbers of people have found an adequate functional substitute for marriage, yet a smaller percentage of adults are married, and marriage seems not to be serving the needs of married persons as well as it once did.

If this picture is even roughly accurate, there is reason for concern, not only because recent trends have negatively affected the well-being of adults, but also because of the likely impact on the welfare and socialization of children. And if there should be a continuing downward trend in how well marriage serves the psychological needs of adults, a widespread psychological and cultural retreat from marriage would seem to be inevitable in the long run. I do not know what the social costs of such a change would be, but I suspect that they would be considerable.

Unfortunately, the downward trend in marital success is likely to be self-perpetuating, regardless of what the specific reasons for it may be. As people begin to perceive how low the probability of success in marriage has become, it will become increasingly difficult for them to totally commit themselves to their marriages and to make the investment of time, effort, energy, and forgone opportunities that a total commitment entails. And without such a commitment, marriages are unlikely to succeed.

The reasons for the changes shown above are undoubtedly multiple and complex, and I cannot deal with all of the possible reasons here. Such changes as increases in expectations of marriage and in the ambiguity of marital roles are almost certainly responsible to some degree, but I suspect that the most important reason is a weakening of the ideal of permanence in marriage and of other values supportive of marriage. Any such value change cannot be measured very precisely by social surveys, and in any event, there is a dearth of comparable data on the topic gathered over the past few years or decades by American national surveys.[25] However, there is considerable indirect evidence of such change, and there have been some unmistakable influences that by themselves should have promoted it. For instance, since the early 1970's, many books and magazine articles have encouraged people to put "personal growth" and self-actualization above permanence in marriage, and some mental-health professionals have quite explicitly encouraged divorce in the case of "stultifying" and "destructive" marriages. The human potential movement, some varieties of feminism, and so-called "progressive" family social science have also contributed to a weakening of the ideal of marital permanence, although it is hard to tell just how widespread and effective their influence has been, and they may have primarily reflected rather than caused value change.

In any event, there apparently has been substantial movement in recent years toward what Bernard Farber has called "permanent availability."[26] This is the condition whereby married persons remain tentatively on the marriage market, being susceptible to being lured out of their present marriages if opportunities for more favorable ones should arise. Although many contemporary marriage ceremonies include traditional marriage vows such as "till death do us part" and "as long as we both shall live," it is doubtful that most brides and grooms really mean what they say. In many cases, more honest vows would be "as long as we both shall love" or "as long as no one better comes along."

Many commentators on contemporary American marriage point to a decline in adherence to the ideal of marital permanence as a reason for an increase in divorce, but many of these same authors deny that this value change has made marriages any less satisfactory. Rather, they are among those I refer to above who believe that the increase in divorce is largely just a matter of people being less willing to tolerate unsatisfactory marriages.

I present evidence above that is inconsistent with this overall view of the increase in divorce, and there are strong theoretical reasons for thinking that a decline in the ideal of marital permanence will tend to make marriages less satisfactory, not just less stable. For instance, the person who enters a marriage with the notion that he or she may remain in it only for a few years will not be inclined to fully commit or to make the kinds of investments that would be lost if the marriage should end. And if a person constantly compares the existing marriage with real or imagined alternatives to it, the existing marriage will inevitably compare unfavorably in some respects. People are hardly aware of needs that are currently being well served, but they tend to be keenly aware of needs that are not being satisfied. And since attention tends to center on needs that are not being especially well met in one's marriage (and there always are some), the grass will always tend to look greener on the other side of the marital fence. Therefore, merely contemplating alternatives to one's marriage may engender marital discontent.

Furthermore, persons who still strongly adhere to the ideal of marital permanence may be afraid to commit strongly to their marriages if they perceive a general weakening of the ideal. Indeed, when the probability of marital success is as low as it is in this country today, to make a strong, unqualified commitment to a marriage, along with the investments that entails, is so hazardous that no totally rational person would do it. To illustrate, many women who made such commitments 20 to 30 years ago are the impoverished "displaced homemakers" of today, and many persons, both men and women, have suffered emotional trauma that would have been less severe if their commitments to their marriages had been more tentative.[27]

I cannot treat in detail here the views of all commentators on American marriage who take a more sanguine view of it than I, but I will mention two for which I have respect in spite of my partial disagreement with them. One of these is the belief that the 1970's and 1980's have been a transitional period of marital instability between the breakdown of the traditional consensus, or near consensus, on marital roles and the emergence of a new near consensus. According to this view, once husbands and wives can reach a new and more equalitarian division of household duties, child-care responsibilities, and decision-making authority, we will enter a new era of relatively stable and satisfactory marriages.

The recent conflicts over gender role issues *have* affected many marriages, but I believe that contemporary marriages are plagued by more fundamental problems that will not be resolved by husbands' and wives' agreeing on more equalitarian marital roles. Furthermore, I doubt that gender-role issues will soon be resolved, especially outside of the rarified upper-middle-class social circles in which most journalistic and academic observers of marriage reside.

The second view worthy of mention is that the stability and quality of marriages depend in large measure on the ratio of males to females among those persons available for marriage.[28] According to this view, when that ratio is low, as it is when those born during a period of rising fertility reach adulthood (because males tend to become available for marriage at a later age than females), males will tend to take advantage of their favorable "market situation" by seeking sexual gratification without the responsibilities of marriage and by making only weak and tentative commitments to their marriages when they do marry. When the situation is reversed (as it is when those born during a period of declining fertility reach adulthood), males will be highly motivated to marry and will tend to be highly committed to their marriages. Of course, this view is based on the old belief that females are naturally monogamous while males are not.

The fact that the divorce rate started to climb steeply as the early baby boomers reached adulthood is consistent with this view, but if the marriage-market sex ratio were the only strong influence on the stability of marriages, the divorce rate should have turned downward after the late baby boomers (born after 1957) began to reach marriageable age. The divorce rate did level off shortly after the late baby boomers became an appreciable proportion of those on the marriage market, so although the marriage market sex ratio can hardly be the only strong influence on marital stability, it may be one among several.

The changed marriage-market sex ratio, the AIDS scare, some resolution of gender role conflict, and several such possible influences may tend to make marriages more successful in the next few years. I doubt, however, that they can effect a major turnaround of the "retreat from marriage." I do not know what would bring about that change, but a necessary condition for it to occur is probably widespread public concern about the individual and social costs of marital failure.

— *Norval Glenn is Ashbel Smith professor of sociology at the University of Texas at Austin.*

ENDNOTES

[1]*John Scanzoni,* Shaping Tomorrow's Family: Theory and Policy for the 21st Century *(Newbury Park, CA: Sage Publications, 1983).*

[2]*By selecting this focus I in no sense mean to minimize the importance of marriage in serving the needs of children or of the society as a whole, nor does this focus mean that I think that American marriage should be as hedonistic as it is.*

[3]*This question has been asked on each of the General Social Surveys (conducted by the National Opinion Research Center at the University of Chicago) since 1973, and a survey has been conducted each year since then except in 1979 and 1981. Each survey sampled, and interviewed face-to-face, about 1,500 respondents selected to represent the English-speaking noninstitutionalized population age 18 and older of the 48 contiguous United States.*

[4]*Responses to the question apparently can be affected by the respondents being asked certain other questions earlier in the interview. Standard practice on the General Social Survey has been to ask the question immediately after a battery of questions on satisfaction with various aspects of life and immediately before a question on global happiness. However, for all or part of the samples in 1980, 1985, and 1986, the*

usual order of the questions was changed (Tom W. Smith, Unhappiness on the 1985 GSS: Confounding Change and Context *[Chicago: NORC, 1986]). In compiling the data for this paper I at first excluded the data for those years, but the patterns shown differed in no important way from those in Tables 1 through 8, in which the data from all of the surveys are included.*

[5]*The indicated change for both males and females is statistically significant (for males, $p < .01$, and for females, $p < .05$) on a two-tailed test. (In applying significance tests, I multiplied the standard errors computed by the formula designed for simple random samples by 1.3 to take into account the multi-stage cluster design of the samples.)*

[6]*The number of divorces per year per 1,000 married women age 15 and older increased steadily through the 1970's, going from 14.9 in 1970 to 22.8 in 1979 (U.S. Department of Commerce, Bureau of the Census,* Statistical Abstract of the United States, 1988 *[Washington, DC: U.S. Government Printing Office, 1987], p. 83). Since 1979 the divorce rate has declined slightly, but apparently only because of compositional changes in the population and not because couples at each duration of marriage have become less inclined to divorce (Teresa C. Martin and Larry L. Bumpass, "Recent Trends in Marital Disruption,"* Demography *26 [February 1989]: 37-51).*

[7]*Andrew Greeley, "The Declining Morale of Women,"* Sociology and Social Research *73 (January 1989): 53-58.*

[8]*For evidence on and discussion of this issue, see Norval D. Glenn, "Duration of Marriage, Family Composition, and Marital Happiness,"* National Journal of Sociology *3 (Spring 1989): 3-24.*

[9]*The decline would probably be shown for all durations were it not for sampling error. Most of the differences between the earliest and the latest percentages fall short of statistical significance, but the consistency of the direction of the indicated changes provides strong evidence that declines occurred in the population.*

[10]*Widowed persons had to be excluded in the absence of any information on the quality of the marriages of those who had never been separated or divorced.*

[11]*Most of the indicated changes in Table 3, in contrast to those in Table 2, are statistically significant.*

[12]*For relevant evidence, see Glenn, "Duration of Marriage, Family Composition, and Marital Happiness."*

[13]*For evidence on and discussion of this issue, see Norval D. Glenn and Charles N. Weaver, "The Changing Relationship of Marital Status to Reported Happiness,"* Journal of Marriage and the Family *50 (May 1988): 317-324.*

[14]*The data are restricted to a narrow age range to avoid confounding the effects of marital status with those of age or birth cohort. The 25-39 range is used because there are few never-married persons at older ages, and being never-married is normative below about age 25. The trends shown by data for the total adult population are in the same direction as those shown in Table 4, but are less pronounced.*

The decline in the difference between never-married and married persons shown in Table 4 is statistically significant for males at the .05 level on a two-tailed test and approaches significance for females.

[15]*The indicated decline in the reported happiness of young married women approaches, but does not quite attain, statistical significance at the .05 level on a two-tailed test. Andrew Greeley ("The Declining Morale of Women") reports that most of*

the recent decline in the happiness of young married women has been among mothers working outside of the home. A possible reason for this decline is that married working mothers may now be a less select group that includes more women who work because of perceived economic need or social expectations and who lack the stamina and organizational skills to handle the demands of their multiple roles.

[16]*I use running averages rather than the data for each year to smooth out some of the sampling fluctuation.*

[17]*Glenn and Weaver, "The Changing Relationship of Marital Status to Reported Happiness."*

[18]*Both indicated declines are statistically significant on a two-tailed test.*

[19]*For instance, Noval D. Glenn and Charles N. Weaver, "The Contribution of Marital Happiness to Global Happiness,"* Journal of Marriage and the Family *43 (February 1981): 161-168.*

[20]*The lack of consistently high reported global happiness among those who report high marital happiness may result in part from an overreporting of marital happiness.*

[21]*The male-female difference in the differences is statistically significant on a two-tailed test for all three periods.*

[22]*The difference between the level of reported happiness of persons in marriages of low quality and that of persons in each other situation is statistically significant on a two-tailed test for both males and females.*

[23]*Nor is a marriage of mediocre quality better than none at all, if the reports of marital happiness are taken at face value, since most of the respondents who reported less than very happy marriages said that their marriages were "pretty happy."*

[24]*The limited available survey data on this topic support this conclusion, although respondents' reports of how important the goal of a good marriage is to them should not necessarily be taken at their face value.*

[25]*Most survey respondents still say that they believe that marriages should be permanent, but many of these responses apparently do not reflect a strongly held belief. To my knowledge, there are no comparable trend data on this topic for American adults as a whole.*

[26]*Bernard Farber, "The Future of the American Family: A Dialectical Account,"* Journal of Family Issues *8 (December 1987): 431-433.*

[27]*Dissemination of the kind of information reported in this paper may tend to make people fearful of committing to marriage and thus could contribute to the "retreat from marriage." I trust, however, that the informed concern this information can create will more than offset any such effect.*

[28]*Paul C. Glick, "A Demographer Looks Again at the American Family,"* Journal of Family Issues *8 (December 1987): 437-439. The most elaborate formulation of the sex ratio theory is in Marcia Guttentag and Paul F. Secord,* Too Many Women? The Sex Ratio Question *(Newbury Park, CA: Sage Publications, 1983).*

The Ultimate Costs of the Retreat From Marriage and Family Life

by Jack Douglas

"A split, increasing heterogeneity, and an antagonism of the imperative-attributive and imperative convictions of the members of a society mean the shattering, breaking, and disintegrating of its network of social relationship and of its system of sociocultural values. It is like a torn spider's web and, like such a broken web, it ceases to control innerly the conduct and relationships of the members of the society. They become 'free': they lose the clear 'signposts' and guides, showing them what they should do in any special configuration of their relationship to one another and to the values of the society. Their conduct becomes like traffic in a city square with many corners, where no indication is given as to which direction cars must take, what is the right of way, and what is the order of entering and crossing the square. As a result, cars often collide, the air is full of curses of drivers accusing each other, traffic becomes stalled, a general tangle follows. Similar is the situation in a society with ethicojuridicial heterogeneity of its members, or, what is the same, with a split and shattered and tangled network of social relationships and sociocultural values."

— Pitirim A. Sorokin
SOCIAL AND CULTURAL DYNAMICS, vol. II

The loving partnerships we call the family are the foundation of human life. Without the minimal family partnerships, the individuals' senses of selves would never develop the basic dimensions of security, integrity, and independence necessary for human life to continue. Societies differ widely in some of the specific patterns of behavior they institutionalize to express these minimal partnerships among mothers, fathers, and their children, but in all *living* societies, those which are not dying from demoralization and disorganization, these minimal partnerships are the foundation of all the rest of life. Some individuals in any living society may certainly exist and prosper physically without ever having more than an absolute minimum of these minimal family partnerships, but they can do so only by being dependent upon others who have had them, as we see in the case of slaves taken from their families at a very early age and raised by their masters to be obedient servants. These psychic-slaves, now normally called "narcissists" by psychiatrists, seem to be among the most rapidly growing cohorts of our increasingly anti-family, bureaucratic welfare states.

This foundation of human life and its vast importance have been so obvious to most human beings that they have merely taken them for granted, rarely taking any more conscious note of them than they have of the necessities of air, water, food, and so on. As Bryan Strong and Christine DeVault (1986, p. 4) note, "We generally take the family in which we grow up for granted. It is part of the natural backdrop of our lives. . . . This taken-for-granted quality of families is important. It exists only when a family is more or less performing its functions. Only during a crisis — a severe illness, a sudden conflict, unemployment, divorce, or some other incapacitating event — do we notice the roles each person plays and recognize how vital our family and its members are to us."

Whenever societies have been physically or culturally "shattered" by far more powerful or superior ones, as happened to many of the "primitive" societies in the modernist era of the last two centuries, family life has been severely demoralized and disorganized. Then it has been seen as quite problematic and has no doubt become the topic of endless disputes over "social problems" in the terms of the local dialects. A critical challenge to a living culture produces anxiety, stigmatizing hatred and rage against the threat — all-out war. If the challenge is overwhelming, so that the members of the defeated culture begin to despair, they begin to give up their own most cherished moral beliefs and practices — they demoralize their world and then themselves. Family violence, incest, promiscuity, prostitution, rape, sacrilege against the traditional gods and worldly authorities, enraged violence against almost anyone — but especially within the hated in-group — alcoholism, depression, hysteria, and the many other common symptoms of defeat, submission, and despair grow rapidly. At the extreme of these world shatterings, the people become so highly demoralized that their Erotic primings for the creation and love of life die, become repressed, or never develop, and they die out. The Tasmanians are the most famous example of this death of Eros, but a great many social worlds have died or are dying away from the shattering encounter with Western civilization. (It is the failure to recognize this that has probably done more than anything else to lead anthropologists into a thicket of myths about the sex, love, and family lives of "primitives." Fortunately, there are now many fine works being done by ethnohistorians trying to untangle the vastly complex issues of cultural imperialism, cultural surrender, cultural demoralization and despair, cultural assimilation, cultural compromise, cultural seduction, and so on. See, for example, Axtel, 1985; and Clendinnen, 1987. I hope to publish a general analysis of these complex issues in a book on *Primitive Eros*.)

Though I know of no attempt to do the comparative analysis that would be necessary, I suspect that all civilizations at the heights of their cycles of bureaucratic statism experience these progressive demoralizations and disorganizations of family life and, thus, of life in general, though to widely varying degrees depending on the degree of despair felt by those submitted to the gigantic statist Leviathans. The reason for this is simple and so obvious that it has not been noted. The loving partnerships we call the family are the foundation of human life, as I noted at the beginning. When anyone gains enough power by any means to build immense bureaucracies to regulate the lives of the people, then these new forms of power progressively erode, attach, and displace the family power and the general culture on which the very senses of selves of the people depend. The bureaucracies may begin with fervent expressions of intentions to aid the family, but regardless of good intentions, they must wage war on the family in order to build their own power. They do and, if they win, the family is demoralized and disorganized and the senses of self are thus demoralized and disorganized. As a result, at least ultimately, all of life is progressively demoralized and disorganized.

In the throes of its later stages, the truly "wretched ones" of this despairing culture enter *cultural and family bankruptcy*, a condition in which ever more of them can continue to exist and breed *only* by their dependence on outsiders for material and moral sustenance. But, of course, this external dependence allows and encourages ("incentives") the very demoralization and disorganization that is destroying the culture and senses of self and preventing their rebirth through conversion and rededication to a new, living cultural and family ethos. (It is this condition of cultural and family bankruptcy which Daniel Patrick Moynihan, 1986; George Gilder, 1986; and others have analyzed in different ways.) If the shattering spreads, affecting ever more of the population in ever more extreme ways, the will to live — Eros — dies away, resistance to disease falls as despair grows, and depopulation spreads. Whole societies may slowly wither away in this manner and be easily conquered by a virile war bank of Teutons, Huns, Mongols, and such unbureaucratized riffraff.

These Ages of Corruption coming near the end of the dynastic cycles, including the corruption of family life, have been noted since the ancient world. Tacitus contrasted the virile family life of the Teutons, who were dedicated more to Erotic procreation than sexual recreation, with the family decadence of the senatorial class of Romans under the Empire. And, of course, all educated peoples of the West were acutely aware of the intense family love of this class in the Republic in stark contrast with their family decadence in the Empire, until modernist historical amnesia replaced general education. Confucius was so acutely conscious that family life and dynastic power were highly problematic during the Era of Warring States that he argued systematically that all dynastic power must be built on the basic forms of the family itself in order to continue. Succeeding rulers tried to convince their subjects that they were indeed good "fathers of the nation," just as rulers in all civilizations do, but the dynastic cycle continues to this day in China and just about everywhere.

It is precisely this close connection between the ancient regimes and their political rhetorics of familism that made the family a prime target of modernist revolutionaries in their attempts to vault into a blissful Heaven on Earth beyond the bounds of human nature and human history. The first great eruption of modernist revolutionaries, the French Revolution and its aftermath, gave birth to the basic ideas of sexual modernism (Manuel and Manuel, 1979; Billington, 1980; Douglas, 1987) which underlie the subsequent attacks on marriage and the family in the great political "War Over the Family," as Brigitte and Peter Berger (1983) have so felicitiously called this political war in our own time. Almost all of the famous social critics of the Western World for the past two centuries have attacked the "inequality" and "oppression" of marriage, sex and gender roles, and so on in the litany with which we are all so familiar. The great hordes of Marxists and democratic socialists, as well as the more openly visionary communards (Lauer and Lauer, 1983), proclaimed "sexual revolution" to be the precondition of the one and only true social revolution that would transcend history and usher us into Mao's ninth heaven. Now that our social world is ruled by these modernist forces marching under various banners of Bureaucratic Freedom, it is hardly surprising that we are being rapidly liberated from the traditional forms of family life.

The political attacks on the family were launched primarily against marriage and were presented overwhelmingly in terms of the prime moral symbol of the politics of the age, that of freedom or liberty. "Free love" was the slogan, but it meant freedom from the supposed oppression of the bonds of marriage, not those of mother-hood or fatherhood. Marriage is almost always a compromise partnership with very real constraints that at times are quite oppressive. It was much easier to recruit soldiers to the political war against marriage, especially from the ranks of young men with no wives who were anxious to seize both mates and territory, than to seek to "liberate" people from motherhood, or even the more problematic fatherhood. To this day even most male Marxists get queasy over attacking motherhood. God, the arch villain of patriar-chal restraint in the Judeo-Christian tradition, was an easy target. Fatherhood, with memories of patriarchal constraint often tem-pered by love, was harder. Even in America today, motherhood, the ultimate loving partnership, is normally attacked indirectly, in the name of caring for the mother herself by allowing the state crèche to free her from the awful constraints of motherhood, in the name of freedom of choice, gender equality, family planning, procreative freedom, family prosperity and status, and various other political slogans and programs.

The sexual modernists of all stripes strove steadily, a step at a time, to desacralize marriage and turn it into a secular, statist contract. They did so overwhelmingly in the name of the sacred value (for such it was in spite of the protestations of secularism) of "freedom." The prime argument was simple. Many marriages involve suffering. Freeing the individuals to get out of miserable marriages — giving them the sacred right of divorce — will make them and their children happier, and everyone will rejoice to be rid of these social problems. By the turn of the century, the modernists were winning ever more freedom from the previous sacred and secular contractual obligations of marriage. The official divorce rate in the United States had soared to .7 per one thousand people per year. The family supporters were horrified and predicted an age of father-abandoned children, anxiety, insecurities, family poverty, husbandless women, welfare dependency and general misery. The modernists passionately insisted this was all extremist and that the very slow rise in divorce rates (roughly two tenths of one percent per decade) was significant *only* because it showed that greater freedom was bringing greater happiness all around. (See O'Neil, 1967.)

Today, of course, the official divorce rate is roughly 700% greater in the nation as a whole and about 1,000% in the most modernist regions, notably California, that set the pace for the rest of the nation.

This century-long retreat from marriage is now almost a panicky rout of the pro-family people in our trend-setting states where no-fault "nuptials" are increasingly hedged with informal "trial marriages," real-fault property contracts, separate names, separate bank accounts, and separate lives. In California now most young people suffer one soul-rending divorce-abandonment during childhood, one or more "informal marriage and divorce" in their youth before officially getting married, and then two out of three of them get officially divorced. Since many of the "rejects" — that is, those who remain married because they "fail" to find something more "fulfilling" — are miserable in "shell marriages" and crave "transcendence," the "war on marriage" is pretty much over. Most of the newsworthy intellectuals with enough courage to speak up for marriage, timidly suggesting that it may have something going for it, are hard-core feminists who have already established beyond a doubt their bona-fide credentials as anti-familists and are anxious to catch the next wave of publishing best sellers while avoiding the backwash from the millions of disasters they have previously sponsored, if not caused. (The few who come right out and announce that their previous proclamations of anti-marital purity were causes of disaster, as Maxine Schnall did so brilliantly in *Limits*, 1981, are conveniently forgotten through the informal censorship of silence.)

These best-selling "second thoughts" about marital apocalypse are not anti-family in general, and it is their dawning recognition that the "war on marriage" has become a more open, generalized "war on the family" that has made them queasy about taking the next little steps in the great political drift process. The obvious fact is that the "war on marriage" is now little more than a great many "mopping up" political operations — sideshows — of the central theatre of the "war on the family." The only values clearly left to marriage are some of the most genetically primed patterns of human behavior, those of the parent-child love partnerships. All of the serious campaigns are now being waged against these love partnerships. As I noted, most of them are being waged indirectly, rather than frontally. (Indirection is the key to victory in political warfare even more than in physical combat. See Liddell Hart, 1954; and Douglas, 1989.) The assaults are being waged in legislation, education, the media, adjudication, and on all other major fronts in the names of all once-sacred values — liberty, equality, sorority, fulfillment, happiness, love, economic necessity, prosperity, etc.

The most successful assaults are those launched against the erstwhile rights (powers) of fatherhood. Incest and incestuous child sexual abuse are "red hot" headlines, angles, lead-ins, and stories in the news media and in mass education, especially at the so-called "elite universities" where the bureaucrats and pop-journalists are trained. Generalized child abuse by "fathers" comes next in the ratings. It is rarely mentioned that the vast majority of these attacks are by the mothers' boyfriends and by step-fathers. That, after all, would dampen the anti-father, anti-family impact of the stories, since it shows that such abuse is overwhelmingly the result of the great victory of the forces of freedom — divorce and illegitimacy. Never mind that the actual effect has been to stigmatize real fatherhood, especially genetic but also adoptive. The books pouring out of university presses and other "elite" publishers of scientism generalize the attack to all fronts of fatherhood. "Paternalism" is the arch-demon of the forces of freedom and equality. The core image of the "provider and protector" is already replaced by that of the "exploiter and attacker." There is much ado about court decisions possibly restricting in some minute way the total freedom of would-have-been mothers to abort "fetuses" without agreement from the would-have-been fathers, but this only indicates that there are no significant genetic rights of fatherhood. The one right that fathers are gaining more and more is the right to have wages garnisheed and possibly the right to imprisonment for non-support of children in whom they have few or no rights.

The official illegitimacy rate in the U.S. is still only roughly 20%. (Actually, I am only teasing by using a political word like "illegitimacy." I know the real scientific term is "single parenthood," just like all the text-books rightly teach us by rote.) There is still much room for progress, and we're getting there fast. When we combine single-parenting with divorcing, we find that roughly 70% of white children and 90% of black children born in 1980 can look forward to living part of their lives without real or stepfathers. The "war on fatherhood" is going well on all fronts.

That still leaves us with the most impregnable fortress, that of motherhood. The war is raging furiously on all fronts, mostly by indirect attacks, of course. Impregnability may be the most effective assault of all. By divorcing motherhood from sexual intercourse — through "safe sex," "sexual education," and "planned non-parenthood" of all kinds — we are rapidly decreasing the rates of motherhood. When that first wave of assault fails, we can use "free choice" to cancel "unwanted fetuses," thereby aborting many social problems that would otherwise result from unloving mothers. If that fails, the mothers can show their love by choosing a safe, bureaucratically regulated and increasingly state-financed foster-care nursery. We are making very rapid progress in state crèchery, though we still suffer from a terrible crèche-gap in comparison with Moscow. Today roughly one-half of pre-schoolers attend nurseries and six-monthers are among the most rapidly growing cadres of nursery pioneers. Pro-family conservatives like George Bush see the crisis of the crèche-gap and are doing all they can to provide incentives for loving mothers to turn their babies over to bureaucratic strangers. In short, it increasingly pays mothers to trust the statist nannies, who will educate them from their first moments of consciousness in all the scientific vocabularies and ideas about the New Family without marriage, fathers, or even mothers.

In one lifetime the living language of love and family that was built up over eons in the Western World has been largely murdered. Eros, the god of procreatory, creative love, has been turned into "erotic violence" and "S & M" in our college textbooks, because it is politically dangerous to believe that the desire for children, one of the most universal of human urges, can possibly be a result of human nature. (Human nature is now politically censored from almost all social science and humanistic education. See Douglas, 1989.) The phalanxes of Freudians, sexologists, therapists, feminists, and other political shock troops have transformed "love" into a three letter word — "SEX" — and banned procreation and all drives of human nature from sex. (See Douglas and Atwell, 1988.) Very few students at the "elite" University of California now even know enough about the pre-modernist world — the ancient days of fifty years ago — to know that anything has changed. They assume that "erotic" always meant "dirty" or "violent" sex and that the desire for children is merely a remnant of bourgeois "brainwashing." And they believe this and most of the modernist ideologies with passion that often breaks through their facades of "coolness." They are the products, the designer minds, of those school textbooks which Paul Vitz (1985) found had repressed mention of "husband," "wife," and other bits of bourgeois sentimentality and even more of the role models who taught from the texts and who proclaimed the New Family-Think on the television babysitters.

Those social scientists and erstwhile humanists who sincerely believe that there is no human nature, that there is nothing that is essentially "human" and that all of our feelings and thoughts can be designed by central planners of our cultural institutions, do not believe there are any *necessary* costs involved in this rapid erosion and eradication of the ancient cultural patterns of family life. They recognize that there are some short-run costs borne by the victims of their mistakes. After all, they are well aware that the great majority of people today are suffering terribly for some years over their family troubles. (Even popular books such as that by Wallerstein, 1989, now discover this astounding fact, which had been hotly denied by some earlier "scientific" work.) The modernists are also aware that they too have almost always suffered terribly from parental neglects and abandonment, from betrayals and jealousy, from abandonment and divorce, from the unplanned depressions following their abortions, from the awful sufferings of their own neglected and abandoned children, and from the many other tribulations of the true faith in sexual modernism.

But true believers let no such "short-run" catastrophes stand in the way of true faith. It may be true that two-thirds of new marriages in California now end in divorce and even more in hatred and misery, but this only shows the need for more "fine tuning" of the central plans. Presumably, we need not merely "no fault" expropriations of marriage contracts, but "positive no fault" laws; not merely "planned parenthood" and "abortion factories," but "centrally planned and subsidized abortions"; not merely "pre-school education," but "total-development toddler crèches"; and so more and more of the same.

The sexual modernist faith is at the very heart of the more general, absolutist faith of modernism which has triumphed over Christianity and all of the earlier cultural belief systems. One of the monomythic articles of faith of modernists is the Myth of Victorianism (which is a core element of the more general Myth of the Bourgeois). We all know about the evils — the absolute costs of Victorianism unmitigated by benefits — of that awful Victorianism. Victorians were sexually frigid, unloving, child-abusing, child-exploiting, totally immiserated in their marriages and families, forbidden by law to leave this institution of marital slavery, wife battering and whoring, and withal total hypocrites who pretended in their diaries to be happily married and to love their tyrannical parents. Victorians were exactly like Charles Dickens said — or rather, exactly like the scoundrels who dominated between the happy beginnings and happy endings of his syrupy novels. Wives and children were mere slaves — property — and were treated like dirt by the Evil Patriarchs who spent their time prowling the streets of London as Secret Victorians venting their evil passions upon helpless waif-slaves who ran away from their Evil Patriarch fathers who treated them like slave-dirt.

We must always remember that for all true believers in sexual modernism the Myth of Victorianism is above all a litany of the absolute costs of the traditional marriage and family life. And we must always remember that anything we say or do is used to reinforce that litany of absolute costs — evils. In the great world wars which have ravished the modernist era, the "enemies" have always been stigmatized as non-human, and anything they say against the forces of "good" has reinforced the hate-filled stigmatization of themselves. That is how absolutist thinking works in human nature. (Christians, being human beings, were very subject to this same mechanism of absolutist hatred. Thus, whenever the enemy said anything which on the surface sounded good, the good Christian would remind the true believers that "the Devil moves in many and mysterious ways.") In the Great Cultural World War that is now raging between sexual modernists and those of us who make up weak and shifting coalitions of infidels, the same backfire effect is at work. For true believers in sexual modernism there are no ultimate costs in the retreat from marriage and the family — all such "retreats" are really "advances" away from the absolute evils of traditionalistic tyranny — repression, especially in its most awful form, that of paternalistic sexual repression of sexual liberation. There can only be benefits — joyful release — in making progress away from this slough of despair.

A true believer in extreme biological determinism, such as the much loathed Social Darwinists, would also not be too worried by these soaring short-run costs, since they believe human nature will reassert itself in the long run. Unfortunately, almost all of those of us now studying human nature have a more complex view which allows for much more catastrophe than we have already experienced. We agree on the one hand that in the long run when all of us individuals will be dead and buried with John Maynard Keynes, our genes will on average outlive the catastrophes our modernists have planned by mistake. After all, all previous Ages of Catastrophic Corruption were eventually replaced by non-utopian ages of practical wisdom with their conservative modicums of happiness. Tacitus' age of imperial family corruption was eventually replaced by the Dark Ages of relative Christian happiness.

Unfortunately, like good scholars of the ancien régime, we remember that other hand which more than undoes the good done by the one hand. We remember, for example, that Tacitus was writing about the first century A.D. and that things got even worse in the next two centuries before the citizens of the Empire gratefully conspired in its destruction. Is it possible that we have only seen the beginning of the costs of the modernist rout of marriage and family life? Certainly. While recognizing that we can only guesstimate these things with wisdom and a wide margin of uncertainty all around, my own guesstimate is that this is the case for several major reasons. One is Tacitus'evidence — previous imperial bureaucratic states did at times cause progressive, ever more generalized misery for a few centuries before being conquered by more virilely erotic societies. Barring a nuclear comeuppance, we could do the same.

A second and more potent reason for believing that our *via doloroso* will be a long one is that there really are many delightful benefits to this rout of marriage and family life. Most conservatives are so horrified by the obvious long-run costs of sexual modernism that they forget to tote up the many short-run benefits required for a good cost-benefit analysis in the modernist manner. Christians should never forget this, since it is basic to their faith that sin is rampant precisely because it is so exquisitely tempting — it feels much better in the short run than virtue. Any good student of human nature, and any successful bon vivant, must agree, though sometimes for different reasons. The hippies were right — casual sex really is exciting and fun for most people, while marital and family responsibilities are a real drag—in the here-now-this which is everything to the modernist and to most of the young.

Consider, for example, the extreme situation of young men in the so-called welfare ghettoes. Sex is free and easy, cool and casual. Casual sex is rampant, because it has few post-coital costs — responsibilities. The old clichè of street gangs was "Love 'em and leave 'em." The love, of course, is in the modernist, Freudian sense of "*sex*"; and the "leave 'em" is in the far more caring sense of the modernist state of "leave 'em for someone else to pay for and raise in the state hospitals, state housing projects, state crèches, state maximum-security schools, and state prisons." And that's what the most successful of them do, so that the most welfarized of these progressively bankrupted and shattered subcultures have "single parenting" rates of 90% or more. There are vast short-run benefits in this way of life, ranging from orgiastic delights to the welfare benefits of AFDC and many other facilitating and "helping" agencies. Anyone who fails to see how delightful the short-run benefits are has forgotten Christianity, human nature, and what it was like to be young.

Though there are many subcultural and supracultural variations, which add many unwanted short-run costs to this list of delights for most young people, the vast majority of them are moving steadily in the same direction, because the benefit-incentives are moving in that direction. One of the most popular t-shirt and bumper-sticker avowals of faith in California is "Life's a Beach." This means many things to many people — which is the meta-message of the slogans "Do your own thing" and "If it feels good, do it." But the most general list of particulars under the heading of "beach" would be those of "casual living" — everything from casual wear to casual sex at the nude beach. Relax, play it cool, no hang-ups, no regrets, "Love 'em and leave 'em." (It used to be that for each young male who could just "leave 'em" there was one young woman left carrying the costs, but now that cost is increasingly voided at the friendly abortion parlor, where she can exercise her modernist-given free choice over life and death, or it is shifted to the column of the Federal deficit to pay for AFDC, so that even the much abused taxpayer is given the illusion of "free and costless choice.") They have certainly not achieved the casual bliss of the true denizens of the welfare state, but even the minority of yuppies among these young modernists normally share the same sexual ideals, with much less of a tendency to bear the costs of welfare dependent babies. (College girls have been liberated from hang-ups over "free choice" by sex education, so they are immensely more likely to visit the friendly "free choice" parlor next to the campus disco than to give in to the cultural "brainwashing" about the sanctity of life.)

Faced with the same calculus of costs and benefits as our college students are today, how many of us "old geezers" who ponder long-run costs and benefits would give in to the many incentives to "love 'em and leave 'em" in the modernist senses if we were still consumed by the fires in the blood of youth? And how many of us would be tempted to jettison old-fashioned cost-benefit analyses for the delights of the modernist ethos which now envelops most of them from the days of television-transfixed toddlerdom to the plethora of feminist courses on "alternative" living patterns at State U?

Which brings us to an even more potent reason for believing that we shall long be seeing more of the same solution-causes to the same problems. Modernism is now firmly entrenched — institutionalized — in almost all of the elite citadels of our culture, in the mass media, in elementary school, and in the state-regulated crèches. Is there a single professor in the massive University of California teaching the new elites of our media and government bureaucracies that the ancient cost-benefit analyses of family life of Christians, Moslems, Buddhists, or any other living cultural tradition are still true? There are still a few of us who are stigmatized as "crazy conservatives," but I doubt that anyone would be that crazy. Would anyone really dare to teach that the assembly-line abortions at the corner abortion parlor are sins or crimes? Breathes there a journalist with soul so unrehabilitated that he-she would dare to call a champion of "free choice" a "pro-abortion activist" — or even a "pro-baby-slaughter activist?"

No, sexual modernism is now so completely in control of our very language for discussing all of life that almost no *educated* Americans even reacted in shock and horror when our highest courts redefined unborn babies as "fetuses" outside the realm of human beings and human rights. They have a passive knowledge that the abhorred Nazis redefined Jews as subhumans ("*Untermenschen*") to justify aborting their lives, but it never occurs to them that we have gone further down the same path of dehumanization and have done so for our own erstwhile children.

To the dominant political elites in the U.S. today there are no significant costs to the retreat from the Victorian marriage and family. Any short-run costs resulting from mistakes are completely overridden by the supposedly vast benefits of progress, including that prime symbol of modernism — "pro-choice." And by the same calculus, and a totally different, irreconcilable system of values, to us unrehabilitated believers in human nature and the ancient wisdom of human religions and reason, the costs have been extreme. We hide this truth from ourselves by pretending that we share some body of common morality and reason with the modernists who have built this new world and control it. We pretend that we can demonstrate to them with empirical evidence and logical reason that they have produced a catastrophe. We pretend that we can resolve our irreconcilable differences by doing cost-benefit analyses. But this is a false hope.

Consider the prime symbol of modernism — "pro-choice." We could try to document a huge increase in acts of "pro-choice" since the Supreme Court pronounced that the ancient meanings of life were overturned. We could assert that this proves that there are huge costs in human life to this retreat from traditional conceptions of conception itself. So what? They merely assert with aplomb that "human life" does not begin until the first day of the second trimester of . . . "fetusness" or whatever it is up to that moment of non-humanness. Redefinition and checkmate to the traditional cost-benefit analysis. The editors and workaday journalists and writers of all the major news media and the textbook publishers do this rewriting of all thinking in a very systematic, planned, and generally secret way.

On the morning of March 25, 1989, my local newspaper, the very "conservative" Copley Press *San Diego Union*, reports on page 3 that yesterday 350 "anti-abortion activists" sat in front of clinics in Los Angeles to try to prevent their opening. The headline of the story reads, "Pro-choice, abortion foes clash." It mentions that a woman activist held up a "picture of numerous fetuses." Over a year ago that same newspaper ran an editorial exposing a letter sent out by New York editors, including one at the *New York Times*, urging all editors to use the language approved by the "pro-choice" people (without noting that seminal fact). They now use the accepted language. So much for "conservatism."

Of course, there is nothing new in this expropriation of traditional language to destroy tradition. The methods of New Speak were standardized in the redefining of "liberal" as one who supports government power. The Soviets invented the word *"agitprop"* to talk about such methods, but really effective political actors do not invent words to expose their own machinations. It was not the Borgias or even the Medicis who invented Machiavellianism as a word — in fact, Lorenzo refused even to acknowledge receiving a copy of the book, presumably understanding that silence is the best tactic for creating a "non-person," and Machiavelli himself, though obviously insane, was not crazy enough to publish the book while alive. Modernist *agitprop* is never called by its name and, in fact, educated Americans do not even know what *agitprop* means — since we obviously do not have any.

The crucial point is that the catastrophic costs of the retreat from marriage and family life can only be felt or seen by those who share the same values, language, and methods of reason. We who still share the values of the now stigmatized "traditional" family life cannot demonstrate to modernists the long-run catastrophes of their ways by adopting their language and methods of pseudoscientific reasoning *which were created for the purpose of insinuating and supporting their values against the very family values we share.* It is quite true, for example, that all significant evidence reveals that the unmarried suffer far more from numerous diseases and misfortunes, including earlier deaths. It is also true that the present government programs do and will bear monetary costs running into the tens of billions a year because of these diseases and other misfortunes. (Bryce Christensen, 1988, has summarized major findings concerning these monetary costs.) By focusing on these monetary costs we can probably dissuade a few legislators still wavering from joining the True Modernist Faith.

I believe it is true, though less empirically verifiable at this time, that there are even more immense costs involved in this headlong rush into anti-familism. As I noted at the beginning, the war on the family has been centered on the war on marriage until recent decades. Now motherhood itself is under some direct attack and much more extensive indirect attacks. No one today would say that anything is "as uncontroversial as apple pie and motherhood." Apple pie is under attack as a source of alar-induced disease, and motherhood is under attack as an awful constraint on total freedom, self-fulfillment, and much more. There is a mass of evidence, ranging from our commonsensical observations to the works of John Bowlby (1969-1980) and many others, indicating that the mother-child love partnership is absolutely vital to the development of the independent, secure, and integrated sense of self of the adult human being. (See the general theory of insecurity and security presented in Douglas and Atwell, 1988.) Bowlby (1986) has estimated that in Britain some years ago nearly one-third of adults were already basically insecure, mainly because of disturbances in the ancient patterns of mother-child partnerships. Though any pretense of quantitative precision in such matters would be pseudo-science, my guesstimate would be that there are many more than this now in our nation, especially in the great centers of "progress" like California. Tens of millions of people are "keeping it together" or "keeping on top of it" to a minimally functional degree only by living on maintenance doses of designer poly-drug addictions (mostly by medical prescription), alcohol, innumerable brands of psychotherapy, neo-cultism, welfare dependency, neo-hermetism, neo-monasticism (shelters of various kinds), and other brands of dependency. In this age of modernist liberation, *dependency* is in fact the exploding reality — drug dependency, therapy dependency, cult dependency, government dependency, political-addiction dependency, and so on and on. These dependencies are iron shackles of the soul itself. The modernist he-she is not only a social animal, but a domesticated and caged animal with an immensely insecure and fragmented sense of self which can live only by dependency on the shrinking number of independent zoo keepers.

I suggest, however, that by doing any such modernist cost-benefit analysis we have in fact joined the modernist enterprise — obviously unintentionally. All good things have financial costs. The fragrance of the spring's rose costs money to buy the rose bush, feed it, and so on. Raising a child is very expensive indeed. Having a baby costs more than a quickie exercise of "pro-choice." Think how much we would save by planning away all procreations — or by merely limiting each adult to one-half of an offspring per lifetime, roughly as the Central Committee of Freedom and Equality now does in the People's Republic of China? Suffering? Did the hundreds of thousands of American casualties in World War II mean that we should have refused to fight? The real American liberals proclaimed, "Give me liberty or give me death." Should we expect modernist liberals to retreat from the glories and other inherent values involved in "pro-choice" and "creative divorce" because there are some bits of paltry suffering involved in choosing the morally right path to freedom and fulfillment? Insecurity? Did the early Christians increase the sense of secular security by announcing the impending end of the world? Were Christians not dependent on God as their "Rock of Ages"?

Let us not underestimate the modernists. These are very serious, very intelligent — often brilliant — courageous, creative, and morally impassioned he-shes. They are marching resolutely to the Neo-Zion, to the best of punk rock. They know that all truly good things in life cost money and involve some pain — life is a matter of trade-offs, as the neo-classical economists assure us. The exercise of free choice in the friendly abortion clinic can cost several hundred dollars. But mass production techniques and price controls regulated by a new Federal Department of Biological Freedom could bring the cost down dramatically, bringing freedom within the reach of millions more. Pain and depression? New technologies, new designer drugs, government financed maintenance doses, and so on can solve the problems. Whoever said that freedom is painless? Whoever said that morality is painless?

Most of the pro-family people do not even know that the sexual modernists have declared a cultural war on them involving all the massive armory of *agitprop*. Brigitte and Peter Berger actually named their book *The War Over the Family: Capturing the Middle Ground*. They see it as mainly an intellectual argument, not a political war, and seek to compromise the way all good citizens of community-loving democracies do. Maybe a compromise in which our abortions were cut in half to a *mere* 650,000 a year, our divorce rate to a mere 2.5 per thousand married women per year, and so on would be better than what we have. Somehow, I don't think that is what the warring parties have in mind. Maybe in the end they will be forced to a compromise, as Christian rulers were so forced to compromise by the immense death and destruction of the Thirty

Years War, but it is not the voice of reason or cost-benefit analyses done by the calculus of modernism that will force such compromises.

My own experience has been that the sexual modernists are still on the march. They have all the political high ground — the legislators, the executives, the courts, the schools, the "elite" universities and mass media. They dictate the language that can be used in published and broadcast debate. They are always willing to compromise our own position, to slice off a bit more of what is ours, while holding on firmly to what is theirs. They are scientists of the first order and are always willing to engage in cost-benefit forays, as long as the language, rules of analysis, official statistics, and so on are controlled by them.

The important questions, and the ones we should be concerned with in all our initial arguments, are those of ultimate truths, ultimate values, and ultimate costs. Is there a human nature? Are there basic moral values inherent in marital and family love? Is marriage a sacrament or an arbitrary social contrivance? Is freedom of choice so valuable that it outweighs the moral values of motherly love? Are first-trimester unborn babies really babies — human beings who have done nothing morally wrong? Or are they mere protoplasmic flotsam — fetuses — to be vacuum-cleaned away like dirt on the living room rug? Is abortion baby murder, baby slaughter, or courageous free choice? Did slavers have the right to redefine African slaves as "inferior beings" beyond the realm of Christian values? Did Nazis have the right to redefine Jews as *"Untermensch"* beyond the realm of Christian and legal values? Do we have the right to choose to redefine and execute any group we wish because free choice is so absolutely right? Do feminists or Chinese Communists have the right to redefine human life or the rights over life? Do convicted mass murderers have the right to a tax-financed lifetime in prison, while unborn babies have no rights to life at all, as American liberals proclaim today? Is the secure, integrated, and independent sense of self of value in itself, or are dependency on drugs, therapy, and government zoo maintenance of greater value? Is motherhood an ultimate fact and value of human life or a mere social convention? Are motherhood, fatherhood, and childhood ultimate fulfillments of human life, or is the yuppie career climbing the labyrinthian rungs of the local government bureaucracy the ultimate fulfillment?

These and many more are the important questions and the answers to them the foundations on which all else depends. Those of us who share some variations on the ancient answers given to them in all civilizations, except at the awful peaks of their cycles of dynastic bureaucratization, know very well that our society has been experiencing a catastrophic rise in personal costs — misery and tragedy — because the retreat from family life is inherently miserable and tragic and because it immiserates the rest of life as well. It does not even occur to us that we could get rich by selling our children to yuppie women who forgot that nature decrees a time for all things in life — so how could we do a modernist cost-benefit analysis of it? It does not make the least bit of rational sense to us that anyone could even think they have a right to choose to kill any innocent person — and the idea that a mother could possibly have a right to murder her own unborn, totally innocent baby is insane. When Jews start doing cost-benefit analyses of the Nazi Holocaust, then we should start doing cost-benefit analyses of the American Holocaust. Until then we must recognize that questions of the ultimate good and evil cannot be answered by an economic calculus and that they are the serious questions that confront us and must be answered in this war over the foundations of all human life before any rational discussions can begin.

— Jack Douglas is professor of sociology at the University of California-San Diego.

REFERENCES

Axtel, James. The Invasion Within. *New York: Oxford University Press, 1985.*
Berger, Brigitte, and Peter Berger. The War Over the Family. *Garden City, New York: Doubleday, 1983.*
Billington, James. Fire in the Minds of Men. *New York: Basic Books, 1980.*
Bowlby, John. Attachment and Loss. *New York: Basic Books, 1969-1980, 3 vols.* The Making and Breaking of Affectional Bonds. *London: Tavistock Publications, 1986.*
Christensen, Bryce J. *"The Costly Retreat from Marriage,"* The Public Interest, *Spring 1988, Number 91, pp. 59-66.*
Clendinnen, Inga. Ambivalent Conquests. *New York: Cambridge University Press, 1987.*
Douglas, Jack D. *"The Sexual Modernists,"* The Family in America, *Vol. 1, May, No. 3, 1987. And Freda Cruse-Atwell,* Love, Intimacy and Sex. *Beverly Hills, Califor-*

nia: *Sage Publications, 1988.* The Myth of the Welfare State. *New Brunswick, New Jersey: Transaction, 1989.*

Festinger, Leon, Henry W. Riecken, and Stanley Schachter. When Prophecy Fails, *New York: Harper, 1964.*

Gay, Peter. The Bourgeois Experience. *New York: Oxford University Press, Vols. I and II, 1984-1986.*

Gilder, George. Men and Marriage. *Gretna, Louisiana: Pelican Publishing Company, 1986.*

Hart, B.H. Liddell. Strategy. *New York: Praeger, 1960.*

Lauer, R.H., and J.C. Lauer. The Spirit of the Flesh. *Metuchen: The Scarecrow Press, 1983.*

Manuel, Frank E., and Fritzie P. Manuel. Utopian Thought in the Western World. *Cambridge, Mass.: Harvard University Press, 1979.*

Moynihan, Daniel Patrick. Family and Nation. *San Diego: Harcourt, Brace, 1986.*

O'Neill, William. Divorce in the Progressive Era. *New Haven, Conn.: Yale University Press, 1967.*

Schnall, Maxine. Limits. *New York: Potter, 1981.*

Strong, Bryan, and Christine DeVault. The Marriage and Family Experience. *Los Angeles: West Publishing Company, 1986.*

Vitz, Paul. "Textbook Bias Isn't of a Fundamental Nature," The Wall Street Journal, *December 26, 1985.*

Wallerstein, Judith, and Sandra Blakeslee. Second Chances. *New York: Ticknor and Fields, 1989.*

'Love in the Ruins'? The Future of Marriage in Modern America

by Bryce J. Christensen

My title is borrowed from the distinguished Catholic novelist Walker Percy, whose novel *Love in the Ruins* (1971) offers an imaginative look at marriage "at a Time Near the End of the World." Appearing as the protagonist, the Louisiana psychiatrist Thomas More has lost his first wife, who "ran off with a heathen Englishman and died on the island of Cozumel" before the novel begins. During the course of the novel, Dr. More tries to decide which of three women (Lola Rhoades, Moira Schaffner, or Ellen Oglethorpe) to marry or whether — with polygamous Abraham as his precedent — to marry all three. In any case, Dr. More feels few social pressures in making his decision. In Percy's imagined future, American society has fractured into irreconcilable fragments — Christian Knotheads, Lefts, drugheads, Ku Klux Klan, liberals, black Bantu guerrillas — bound together by few shared beliefs. The sanctity of marriage does not count as one of those shared beliefs. Percy depicts a world so uninhibited in sexual mores that a Catholic priest gladly helps conduct studies of copulating volunteers, while one of Dr. More's colleagues regards his self-accusing use of the word *fornication* both as an anachronism and as a symptom of mental imbalance.[1]

While a novelist can provide neither statistical precision nor theoretical rigor, he can provide a vista of imaginative possibility for considering the future of marriage. Percy's imaginative vista has arguably grown less implausible in 1989 than it was in 1971. Few Americans now find themselves in anything resembling Dr. More's marital circumstance, but marriage has become remarkably problematic in recent years, with every indication that it will grow more so. Outside of some religious communities, social sanctions against divorce and premarital intercourse have almost disappeared.

Simultaneous polygamy of the sort contemplated by Dr. More can be found only in a few isolated communities of excommunicated Mormons in the Southwest, but millions of Americans now practice what has been called "serial polygamy" (i.e., short-term marriage to a series of spouses).[2] Over four million Americans now live in nonmarital cohabitation, while living alone is the lifestyle of preference for millions more.[3] According to recent surveys, 25 to 50 percent of married women and 50 to 65 percent of married men now have at least one adulterous relationship during their lives.[4] And a recent history of prostitution finds that American streetwalkers are finding it increasingly difficult to make a living, because American men now find it so easy to find women willing to engage in casual sex for free.[5] Even "the love that dare not speak its name" (Oscar Wilde's famous characterization of homosexuality) has come out of the closet, militantly accusing all its foes of "homophobia."

On the other hand, enduring marriage has never been less common in American history. Since 1970 the American marriage rate has dropped 30 percent among unmarried women ages 15 and over, while the divorce rate has climbed 50 percent.[6] The average age for first marriage has climbed to 26.8 for men and to 24.5 for women. One American in eight now remains unmarried for life. Surveying the statistics, demographer Robert Schoen discerns a "continuing retreat from marriage" over the past two decades. Schoen even wonders if we are not witnessing "a fundamental change in the nature of marriage."[7] Thomas Espenshade of The Urban Institute has similarly concluded that "marriage is weakening as a social institution in the United States."[8] Stanford scholar Kingsley Davis concurs: "A weakening of marriage is certainly occurring, at least in the sense that matrimony is rapidly becoming less prevalent."[9] Officials at the National Center for Health Statistics report that since 1970 "the status of marriage in America" has been in "steady decline," as "a rising share of eligible people are choosing not to marry."[10]

Some of the forces causing this retreat from marriage appear obvious; others are harder to identify. A number of profound cultural developments, stretching back over at least two centuries, have rendered marriage both less attractive and more difficult to maintain. Patterns of American life long defined by religion, agriculture, and community tradition have slowly been displaced by secular, urban, commercial, and individualistic variants. As early as 1861, the great British jurist Henry Sumner Maine saw how modern life in the Western World was uprooting the binding "status" relationships of kinship and reordering society on the basis of "contract," relationships entered by choice for temporary mutual benefit. Maine traces this development succinctly: "Starting, as from one terminus of history, from a condition of society in which all the relations of persons are summed up in the relations of Family, we seem to have steadily moved toward a phase of social order in which all these relations arise from the free agreement of individuals."[11]

Since the Industrial Revolution of the late 1700's, the family has surrendered ever more of its educational and economic functions to the state or to the marketplace. The normative authority of marriage has naturally suffered in this realignment.

Despite these long-term trends, however, Davis is right to insist that "compared to most other aspects of human society, marriage has changed surprisingly little" since the late 1700's. Indeed, Davis supposes that "the weakening of marriage as an institution" did not become particularly pronounced in the United States until the end of World War II.[12] Even the sudden eruption of divorce that occurred during the late 1940's might be partially explained as an aberration, an aftereffect of the war that was quickly erased by the fervid domesticity of the 1950's. Contemporary sociologists need look no further back than the early 1960's to find "relatively early and widespread marriage, relatively low divorce rates, and relatively high fertility" in the United States.[13]

In retrospect, though, the remarkable blooming of marriage and family during the 1950's was largely a cut-flower illusion. After a decade and a half of depression and war, Americans were eager to spend their newly won prosperity in a family way, but were not willing to reverse the deep-seated historical forces that were eroding the family's place in society. As unbelief, modernity, and consumerism continued to rise during the 1960's, any reasonable observer could have predicted a slow, steady fading of marriage and family life in America. But America has witnessed a far faster unraveling of marriage and family than can be explained simply by extrapolating pre-1960's trends. By the late 1960's and early 1970's, identifiable new forces were grievously exacerbating the long-term trends. Particularly deserving attention are five new influences, all of them either engendered or emboldened by imprudent government actions.

Beginning with the founding of *Playboy* in 1963, the publishers of "girly" magazines and of hard-core pornography began a surprisingly strong and effective attack upon marriage. In his very first issue of *Playboy*, editor Hugh Hefner emphasized that "we aren't a 'family magazine.'" Subsequent issues repeatedly ridiculed marriage as a "bondage of breadwinning" and an impediment to sexual fulfillment.[14] In *The Rape of the A*P*E* (American * Puritan * Ethic), published in 1973 by Playboy Press, Allan Sherman chronicled the "obscening of America" and the passing of the "incredibly clean-cut and impossibly wholesome" American culture of the 1950's. After the sex revolution which *Playboy* helped foment, "nothing was reduced to less recognizable rubble than the revered ... Institution of Marriage." In fact, Sherman boasted that by 1973 "it was getting increasingly difficult to explain why marriage was necessary at all."[15] Much more recently, Christie Hefner — daughter of Hugh Hefner and now president of Playboy Enterprises — has justified her own place in the feminist movement by arguing that *Playboy* helped pave the way to feminism by pioneering the rebellion against oppressive and restrictive family roles. "The things *Playboy* really believes in," she affirms, "are the same kinds of ideals that have been embraced by most of the progressive movements, including the women's movement." Christie Hefner counters the hostile views of those feminists who consider *Playboy* an "enemy" by pointing out that in the early 60's "*Playboy* was the most influential force in mass communications and in financing for the revolution in abortion laws and birth control."[16]

In a major Justice Department study of pornography, Judith Reisman argues that the eroticism found in *Playboy* — and *Penthouse* and *Hustler* — has grown more violent over the last 30 years and less respectful of the distinction between adults and children. In her view *Playboy* has helped foster a cultural climate of "mutual distrust" and "heterophobia" between the sexes.[17] Perhaps government censorship could not have put *Playboy* out of business (though Hugh Hefner at first feared that possibility), but a 1966 Supreme Court ruling made it very difficult for local authorities to ban even hard-core obscenity. In the case of *A Book Named "John Cleland's Memoirs of a Woman of Pleasure"* v. *Attorney General of Massachusetts* (popularly known as the "Fanny Hill" case), the court articulated a "three-pronged value" test for obscenity cases, ruling that in order for any material to be banned as pornographic, prosecutors had to show that: 1) it appeals to prurient interests; 2) it is patently offensive; 3) it is "utterly without redeeming social value." Prosecutors soon learned that the third prong, the "redeeming social value" test, made it almost impossible to stop the flood of smut.[18]

The Supreme Court did partly rehabilitate anti-obscenity ordinances in 1973 in *Miller* v. *California* by abandoning the "redeeming social value" test and by giving local officials authority to ban materials offensive to "contemporary community standards." But many states which revised their obscenity laws to pass judicial muster in the late 1960's have not yet removed the debilitating "redeeming social value" test, despite the Supreme Court's rethinking of the issue. Even when state legislators have caught up to Supreme Court theory, local officials are finding that — once released — the pornographic genie is not easily pushed back into the bottle. In almost all areas, pornography is far more prevalent today than in 1965.[19]

Even as court-induced paralysis prevented officials from stopping the flood of pornographic pollution, radical environmentalists were lobbying government leaders to protect the country's forests and wildlife against the unrestrained fertility of traditional families. In an era of rising concern about "the population bomb," few policymakers could see reasons for giving tax benefits to families. Some even advocated deliberately antinatal changes in the tax code.[20] Between 1960 and 1984, while the tax rate remained essentially flat for singles and childless two-earner couples, one-earner couples with two children saw their Federal taxes rise by 43 percent, while one-earner couples with four children witnessed a phenomenal 223 percent hike.[21] This unprecedented shift in tax responsibility occurred at the very time that the traditional family was also paying markedly higher payroll taxes for Social Security. Since Social Security actually favors the deliberately childless at the expense of parents, the system further discourages marriage, childbearing, and family life.[22]

Government policy during the 1960's and 1970's not only weakened marriage by taking in money, but also by giving it out. The dramatic growth of the welfare system since the early 1960's has made marriage appear unnecessary to many single women. Charles Murray has argued that current welfare benefits may actually encourage women *not* to marry.[23] Recent studies have found that welfare benefits actually seem both to inhibit new marriages and to weaken existing ones. Family sociologists Randal Day and Wade

C. Mackey believe that current welfare policies encourage the formation of "the mother-state-child family," while weakening the traditional family. In the welfare state, they point out, married fathers must "pay directly for their own children and, in addition, must pay a heavy tax burden to underwrite the state, as the state takes the role of the supportive 'traditional father'" for the children of unwed and divorced mothers.[24]

These economic pressures can hardly foster marriage. One 20-state study found that the higher the available welfare payments, the lower the rate of remarriage among divorced women.[25] Marian Wright Edelman admits the antimarital effects of welfare benefits, although she tries to put the best possible face on the matter: "Welfare — meaning the existence of a bare subsistence grant independent of the man's income — may make women less likely to enter into bad marriages, or more apt to leave ones that have turned bad."[26]

To see how the welfare state fosters a retreat from marriage, it is helpful to consider Sweden, a country widely known for its well-developed and generous welfare system. In a compelling new study of the Swedish welfare state, Professor David Popenoe of Rutgers University reports that the Swedish marriage rate is now "the lowest in the industrialized world," while the rates for nonmarital cohabitation and family dissolution are "probably the highest in the industrialized world." Sweden now has the smallest average household size and highest percentage of single-person households of any Western nation. Popenoe implicates the growth of the Swedish welfare state in the decline of marriage and family life. He even raises the possibility that "the inherent character of the welfare state by its very existence help[s] to undermine family values or familism — the belief in a strong sense of family identification and loyalty, mutual assistance among family members, and a concern for the perpetuation of the family unit." He points out that while many of Sweden's welfare programs "began with the goal of helping families to function better," things did not work out that way: "The very acceleration of welfare-state power weakened the family still further."[27] Allan Carlson has argued that the Swedish welfare state has particularly discouraged marriage through a tax policy that has eliminated the joint return for married couples and has raised marginal tax rates so high that, even through extra effort, a husband cannot support a wife and family on one income.[28]

But growing welfare benefits only partially account for the "divorce revolution" in the United States during the last 20 years. According to one theory, divorce is simply replacing death as the way Americans end their marriage now that they live much longer than their ancestors.[29] This theory might seem plausible for trends between 1900 and about 1960 (although I find it dubious even for that era), but it fails to explain the sharp rise in divorce — much larger than the corresponding fall in widowhood — since then.[30]

Although American divorce rates had been inching up steadily since the turn of the century, they shot up remarkably after the enactment in the early 1970's of innovative "no fault" statutes permitting couples to divorce for no cause other than "irreconcilable differences." In many states, the new laws permitted one spouse *unilaterally* to terminate the marriage without grounds.

Author of a major study on the unintended side effects of no-fault divorce, Lenore Weitzman observes that "a radical change in the rules for ending marriage inevitably affects the rules for marriage itself and the intentions and expectations of those who enter it." No fault divorce, she reasons, is now "redefining marriage as a time-limited, contingent arrangement rather than a lifelong commitment."[31] Sociologist Jack Douglas likewise believes that the new divorce laws discourage women from investing too much emotionally in their marriage or from bearing many children. "These unintended consequences of [no-fault] laws have the further effect of decreasing the bonds of marriage,"[32] he reasons. Adding credibility to this line of analysis is Schoen's prediction that over 40 percent of marriages formed in recent years will end in divorce.[33]

No-fault divorce was only one of the antimarital initiatives promoted by the feminist movement that emerged in the late 1960's and early 1970's. Because they saw in the family "patriarchy's chief institution," feminists launched many attacks on marriage. What began in 1963 with Betty Friedan's fairly restrained complaint that *early* marriage was "regressive" and an obstacle to "women's growth to autonomy"[34] soon amplified into ideological hysteria. In 1971 Germaine Greer indicted marriage for laying the foundations of "the prison of domesticity."[35] "Rape is the first model of marriage," declared Andrea Dworkin in 1975. Dworkin decried the awful pattern of "male domination in Amerika [sic]," where "every married man, no matter how poor, owned one slave — his wife."[36]

The same year, Susan Brownmiller struck a similar chord when she alleged that marriage and rape were "philosophically entwined" and that it was "largely impossible to separate them out."[37]

While extremists in the feminist movement such as Greer, Dworkin, and Brownmiller provided the polemical artillery, feminist foot soldiers carried out a war of attrition in the legislative and bureaucratic trenches. Through a series of Federal measures — the Equal Pay Act of 1963, Title VII of the Civil Rights Act of 1964, the Equal Opportunity Act of 1972, and Title IX of the Education Amendments of 1972 — feminists steered the government away from its traditional posture toward active promotion of sexual egalitarianism. Through the rewriting of school texts, the expansion of girls' and women's athletic programs, creation of affirmative-action programs, and the enactment of antidiscrimination laws, the government vigorously pressed for an unprecedented equality between the sexes.

Despite the defeat of the Equal Rights Amendment, the feminist movement has largely succeeded in abolishing the traditional gender prescriptions that once governed the nation's schools and workplaces. During the 1970's feminism helped to bring record numbers into paid employment, while ensuring that women receive "equal pay for equal work" in their wage competition with men. The new cultural and economic relations between the sexes have profoundly undermined marriage. Davis points out that in the past marriage has rested upon the principle of "complementarity," requiring "a differential commitment to childbearing and child care" and "a division of economic labor, with husband and wife pursuing different activities in the production of goods."[38] The prominent economist Gary Becker corroborates Davis' views in an analysis showing that marriage makes the greatest financial sense when men and women offer one another different kinds of services. In the past, wives have "traded" homemaking and child rearing for a share of their husband's income. In modern America, Becker observes, "the gain from marriage is reduced by a rise in the earnings and labor force participation of women and by a fall in fertility, because a sexual division of labor becomes less advantageous."[39]

A newly feminized capitalism has weakened the economic logic of marriage by putting more women into paid employment and their (usually few) children into day care. At the same time, the new competitive pressures in the wage market have seriously eroded the average man's ability to earn a "family wage" sufficient to support a wife and family. Even Robert S. McElvaine, former speech writer for Walter Mondale, believes that the massive movement of American women into the work force between 1965 and 1980 — at the same time many baby-boomer males were finding their first jobs — was "detrimental to the economy" with "a depressing effect on real income levels."[40] In 1973, almost 60 percent of young men aged 20-24 could earn enough to keep a family of three out of poverty, but by 1984 only 42 percent could.[41]

The harmful effects of female employment upon marriage are especially visible in countries such as Sweden and Denmark, where feminist policies have been in effect longer. Danish demographer Paul C. Matthiessen offers this assessment of why marriage rates have plummeted in Sweden and Denmark while divorce rates have climbed:

The improved economic position of women — a result of their increased participation in the labour force — has probably contributed to the decline in the number of new legal unions (marriages). The woman's earning ability has made marriage less important as a means of support. . . . It is also probable that the woman's improved economic position has contributed to an increase in dissolution of marriages which have failed to meet the expectations of the couples concerned.[42]

Not all of those who have advocated the social, economic, and political changes here surveyed have intended to undermine marriage. Popenoe explicitly discounts the possibility that the architects of the Swedish welfare state were *trying* to undermine marriage and the family. On the other hand, deliberate plans to undermine marriage and the family appear repeatedly in utopian literature, from Plato's *Republic* to B.F. Skinner's *Walden Two*. In such classic works as Plato's *Republic* or Campanella's *City of the Sun*, this utopian assault on marriage and the family is absolute, including plans for communal marriage, eugenic breeding, collectivized child rearing, and virtual abolition of gender differences in dress and occupation.[43] Campanella explains that "self love" will emerge in any regime permitting a man "to use his wife and house and children as his own." "When we have taken away self love," he writes, "there remains only love for the state."[44]

Utopians nearer our own time have usually stopped short of the more radical ideas of communal marriage and eugenic breeding. Still, in *Walden Two* (1948), Skinner does look forward to a time within his imaginary utopian community when "the weakening of the family structure will make experimental breeding possible."[45] More typically, utopians of the last century have reduced marriage to a matter of personal preference, not the foundation of social or economic order. In *A Modern Utopia* (1905), H.G. Wells anticipated a model state with "ample provisions for a formal divorce without disgrace in cases of incompatibility." He even proposed that marriages in utopia could "expire at the end of three or four or five unfruitful years" for childless couples.[46] William Morris went even further in *News From Nowhere* (1891), imagining a model society in which marriage is enshrined in no laws. Instead, disenchanted couples could simply part by mutual consent, as prejudice against illegitimacy evaporates, along with "certain follies about the ruin of women for following their natural desires."[47]

In his *Looking Backward: 2000-1887*, published in 1888, Edward Bellamy anticipated the development of a socialist economy in which "wives are in no way dependent on their husbands for their maintenance," nor are children financially dependent upon their parents, since "it is by virtue of the relation of individuals to the nation, of their membership in it, that they are entitled to support."[48] Wells, Morris, and Skinner also anticipate collectivized economies which end the financial dependence of wives upon their husbands.

For an historical rather than literary illustration of the relationship between utopian aspirations and political delegitimation of marriage, we may consider the family code enacted by the Bolsheviks in the decade after the Russian Revolution. This radical code facilitated easy divorce, abolished the distinction between legitimate and illegitimate birth, enacted broad definitions of what constituted a *family*, gave women greater economic rights in marriage, and provided for state collection of child support. By the mid-1930's, communist leaders had — for pragmatic reasons — largely abandoned these experimental codes and by the 1940's had even partially reinstated the inheritance laws. But the initial Bolshevik codes reveal the *theoretical* antithesis between utopian Marxism and the traditional family.[49]

The imaginative significance of this antithesis is unfolded in *We*, a novel by the Russian author Yevgeny Zamyatin about a totalitarian future in which marriage and the family have been utterly destroyed. Written in 1920-21, *We* could not be published in Russia and its publication abroad in 1924 led to Zamyatin's expulsion from the country. In Zamyatin's anti-utopian novel, the one-party state has so depersonalized its citizens that they are known by numbers, not names. Although reproduction is governed by scientific eugenics, citizens are permitted a libidinal freedom almost as complete as their political slavery. The state proclaims that "each number [i.e., person] has a right to any other number, as to a sexual commodity." Zamyatin depicts this state-sponsored promiscuity as critical to the Party's control of the citizenry, as critical as control of the food supply, since "Love and Hunger rule the World."[50]

Another utopian, Aldous Huxley, has likewise perceived a link between state-sponsored promiscuity and political bondage. "As political and economic freedom diminishes, sexual freedom tends compensatingly to increase," Huxley wrote in 1958.[51] In his own famous novel *Brave New World*, the social engineers governing the utopian state of the future encourage a frenetic but sterile promiscuity. (Children are scientifically conceived and developed in glass bottles.) The only character in the book who believes in continence and marriage is a Savage, raised by his mother on a reservation and educated by reading Shakespeare. Seeking moral purpose and romance, the Savage spins into frustration and rage when brought into the utopian culture of sybaritic regimentation. After the woman he loves dismisses marriage as "a horrible idea" (she had, after all, never seen it practiced) while still offering herself for casual sex, the Savage eventually commits suicide.[52]

How close is contemporary America to an anti-marital utopia of the sort depicted by Huxley or Zamyatin — or even by Bellamy or Wells? Huxley thought we were quite close to his Brave New World in 1947 when he marveled "it looks as though Utopia were far closer to us than anyone, only fifteen years ago could have predicted." As evidence, he noted that "there are already certain American cities in which the number of divorces is equal to the number of marriages. In a few years, no doubt, marriage licenses will be sold like dog licenses, good for a period of twelve months, with no law against changing dogs or keeping more than one around at a time."[53]

Huxley believed this breakdown of American marriage could

well signal a drift toward "the welfare-tyranny of utopia." Just how much closer we have moved since then may be judged by the similarity between the Bolshevik family codes and many American family policies either enacted or seriously contemplated in recent decades.[54] The utopian pressures against marriage may also be gauged by the number of American intellectuals who look to Sweden for political inspiration, quite undeterred by the disintegration of Swedish family life.[55]

Still, America and American marriage may not be Swedenized soon. Religious belief exerts little influence upon Swedish life, according to Popenoe, who finds Swedes much less likely than Americans to accept the judgments of religious leaders and "much more inclined to give legitimacy to the views of social scientists and government experts."[56] Recent international surveys do show a higher proportion of citizens expressing strong religious convictions in the United States than in Europe.[57] Strong religious convictions have been shown to reinforce marriage by reducing the likelihood of cohabitation, illegitimacy, or divorce and by fostering acceptance of traditional gender roles.[58] However, some observers have detected the emergence of "a new denominationalism" in American religious life, most visible in divergent attitudes about family life and sexuality, with Protestant fundamentalists and Baptists strongly conservative; Catholics, Lutherans, and Methodists moderately conservative; Presbyterians moderately liberal; and Jews and Episcopalians distinctively liberal.[59] Because of this emerging denominationalism, the relationship between religion and American family life will probably grow more complex in the future.

In any case, America's cultural and educational elite do not now generally share religious convictions which would reinforce marriage. Rather, many of those who govern what intellectual historian James Billington has called "the university-media complex" espouse views more consonant with utopian designs than with marriage and family life. Billington ventures the judgment that on the question of the family "the values of the American elite" are in fundamental "conflict with the values of the American people as a whole."[60] It should come as no surprise, then, that in a recent survey of social studies textbooks used in America's public schools, psychologist Paul Vitz could find no moral affirmation of marriage or family life.[61]

To understand why the utopian views espoused by many American intellectuals undermine marriage while traditional religious convictions reinforce wedlock, it is helpful to consider an imaginative polarity identified by the Nobel laureate Peter Medawar in his book *The Limits of Science*. "Arcadia," he writes, "is the conception farthest removed from Utopia, for one of its principal virtues is to be pastoral, prescientific, and pretechnological. In Arcadia, mankind lives in happiness, ignorance, and innocence."[62] Medawar borrows the symbol of Arcadia from the Roman poet Virgil, who depicted Arcadia (a district of the Greek Peloponnesus) as the seat of pastoral content. But the imaginative antithesis of Utopia might more properly be identified as Eden, not Arcadia. For in most cases the utopian project begins with the repudiation of Genesis. Among Christians and Jews, Eden stands symbolically opposed to Utopia not only in the ways Medawar has noted for Arcadia, but also in that it constitutes a Paradise lost through the human transgression known as the Fall, cause of mankind's expulsion into a world of sin, adversity, and death. It was in Eden that the God of Scripture ordained the first marriage, and it was at the Fall that He first outlined clear gender roles for husband and wife (see Gen. 2 and 3).

The utopian impulse not only undermines the family, it also blots out consciousness of the post-Edenic realities of death, sin, and guilt. In general, utopians are motivated by a desire to overcome the effects of the Fall without relying on divine redemption. Such utopians wish to "be as gods" (Gen. 3:5) through self-will and human engineering, not through divine grace. To the degree that Americans adopt — consciously or unconsciously — utopian attitudes, to that degree they abandon the moral principles that have undergirded family life since Adam and Eve "hand in hand with wand'ring steps and slow, / Through Eden took their solitary way."[63]

Zamyatin understood well the relationship between Utopia and Eden. Although the sterile glass city of *We* in no way suggests the primordial Garden, the poet R-13 still speaks the truth when he argues that the utopian order strives to make people as "innocent and simple-hearted as Adam and Eve" before they chose "to break the ban [on partaking of the forbidden fruit] and get a taste of ruinous freedom." By stamping out freedom, the One State has triumphed over "the evil serpent" and ended "confusions about good and evil."[64] B.F. Skinner gives away the secret even more candidly when he prompts the founder of *Walden Two* to declare that his design is "rather an improvement on Genesis." Admitting that he "like[s] to play God," this utopian feels that in his attempt to create "a society in which there is no failure," he has done better than God. At least, he asserts, he is disappointed less frequently by his people than God has been disappointed by His children.[65]

It is precisely the utopian's engineered reversal of the Fall which the Savage protests against near the end of *Brave New World.* "I want God, I want poetry, I want real danger, I want freedom, I want goodness. I want sin." Claiming "the right to be unhappy," the Savage affirms also "the right to grow old and ugly and impotent; the right to have syphilis and cancer; the right to have too little to eat; the right to be lousy; the right to live in constant apprehension of what may happen tomorrow; the right to catch typhoid; the right to be tortured by unspeakable pains." In short, the Savage affirms his willingness to live in the post-Edenic world of death and suffering where marriage and family life are desirable and necessary, though difficult.[66]

The utopian's need to repudiate Genesis appears in nonfictional explicitness in the work of New Left philosopher Herbert Marcuse. In his *Eros and Civilization* (1955), Marcuse seeks to advance utopia by directing the imagination away from the fatal consequences of the Fall. Theologians, he complained, "betray the promise of utopia" if they treat death as something other than "a biological fact." Because death constitutes "a token of unfreedom, of defeat," theological or philosophic contemplation on the subject "stifles 'utopian' efforts" and so reinforces "a repressive civilization." The time had come, he urged, to make death "rational, painless. Men can die without anxiety if they know that what they love is protected from misery and oblivion. After a fulfilled life, they may take it upon themselves to die — at a moment of their own choosing." Once out from under the shadow of death, men need no longer accept the restraints of marriage, of gender roles, or of family life. Marcuse asserted that "the gratification of freely developing individual needs" would be achieved in a "non-repressive" society only after the "disintegration of the institutions in which the private interpersonal relations have been organized, particularly the monogamic and patriarchal family."[67]

Because so many Americans (Christians and Jews) profess post-Edenic religious convictions, utopians will probably not soon succeed in establishing a Brave New World in which marriage disappears. However, because many of America's centers of culture, education, and media are in thrall to utopian thinking, marriage will probably cease (if it has not already done so) to define a unifying social norm for the nation. It is true that the social costs of illegitimacy and divorce have given some intellectuals — usually labelled "neoconservatives" — pause to rethink the importance of marriage and the risks of the welfare state.[68] More typically, the problems created by illegitimacy and divorce are cited as reasons to expand the welfare state still further, *not* as reasons to reinforce marriage. For instance, it recently annoyed *Chicago Tribune* columnist Stephen Chapman that the National Commission to Prevent Infant Mortality called in its 1988 report for expanding Medicaid and opening more government-funded clinics, but said nothing about encouraging marriage and personal responsibility.[69] Terry Arendell of the University of California, San Francisco, gives another instance of this kind of thinking when she argues that the negative consequences of divorce justify a radical expansion of welfare services, including "a truly adequate and guaranteed minimum family income," "affordable, high-quality child care programs," "adequate, affordable, and safe housing," and "effective training programs and full employment opportunities for women."[70] It is no wonder that Christopher Jencks recently concluded that marriage rates have fallen among blacks (so creating greater economic dependence upon the welfare state) in large part because the nation's cultural leadership has sent the message that marriage is no longer important.[71]

The breakdown of America's social consensus about the moral significance of marriage quite possibly signals a cultural balkanization, one that bears some resemblance to that depicted in *Love in the Ruins*. Day and Mackey even envision a possible future cultural conflict in America between "two 'tribes,'" families with social fathers vs. families without social fathers. "This tribal fissioning," they speculate, "would probably not be direct. . . . The social dynamics usually operate more indirectly, because the social cleavages caused by different fatherhood roles are most likely to open up along lines already defined by race or religion."[72] At a time when black marriage rates have fallen to only half that found among whites,[73] this line of analysis suggests a possible worsening of race relations in the United States.

Fundamental disagreement about the social significance of marriage could also make the nation's political life more polarized and contentious. The political visibility of "gender gap" issues in recent years has actually obscured a potentially more fundamental political divide: "the marriage gap." Analyst Martin Plissner argues that the marriage gap divides American electorate "more deeply" than the gender gap or the generation gap, noting that married women were more likely to vote for Reagan in 1984 than single men and that while nearly half of those who call themselves Democrats are single, only a third of Republicans are not married.[74] Political scientist Ida Sasser indeed believes that "political activity among poor women in U.S. cities is increasing" because of "a growing dependence on public funds."[75] Noting rather coyly that "an increasing number of women have no husbands to blur their perceptions of their own economic status," Alice Rossi likewise traces growing political activity among unmarried women to their increasing reliance upon "the interlocking strands of the federal safety net."[76]

The increasing frequency of "pro-family" rhetoric by candidates of both major parties can only temporarily obscure the central questions: Should the state reinforce marriage, or should the state expand the social services which make marriage unnecessary? Should the state impose the *value* of marriage, or should it instead impose the collectivized *cost* of repudiating that value? Should public-school educators endorse marriage as a moral norm, or should they simply instruct students in contraceptive technology? If there is any validity to Zamyatin's and Huxley's analysis of the relationship between promiscuity and freedom, then this last issue is of vital importance. In their remarkable retreat from marriage and family life, the Swedes have in fact belatedly learned something of the perils of "welfare-state tyranny": in a survey conducted in 1984, an astounding 81 percent of all Swedes agreed with the assertion that "the state has become increasingly despotic at the expense of individual rights."[77]

Although conservative and religious forces can retard the Swedenizing of America, they cannot effect the cultural and political realignment necessary to restore marriage as a social norm in the foreseeable future. What would restore marriage to normative significance? Popenoe speculates that Swedish trends away from marriage and family life could be reversed through economic decline, a new religiosity, or a national familism campaign.[78] Renewed religious and moral conviction offered the only hope for renewed family life in modern America in the view of Harvard sociologist Pitirim Sorokin. Surveying society in 1957 (during what many now regard as a halcyon era for family life), Sorokin predicted that "the family as a sacred union of husband and wife, of parents and children will continue to disintegrate. Divorces and separations will increase until any profound difference between socially sanctioned marriage and illicit sex-relationship disappears." In Sorokin's view, this trend away from family life could be reversed only by "new Saint Pauls, Saint Augustines, and great religious and ethical leaders." Yet, he did not look to see such leaders until after a time of cultural crisis and upheaval. "By tragedy, suffering, and crucifixion, [society] will be purified and brought back to reason, and to eternal, lasting, universal, and absolute values."[79]

If it is any consolation to those who wish to see a recovery of the sense of marriage as a sacred union, a number of sober observers have recently detected signs of cultural crisis, not only in the United States but in all of Western civilization. In his famous Harvard Address of 1978, Aleksandr Solzhenitsyn decried the state of Western culture as a "calamity" brought on by the repudiation of "the moral heritage of Christian centuries."[80] Less condemnatory towards contemporary culture, Lord Kenneth Clark concludes his essay *Civilisation* (1969) with a wan optimism and a denial that we are entering "a new period of barbarism." Yet, he concedes that "the future of civilisation does not look very bright." As he looks for sources of cultural inspiration, Clark laments that he can find "no alternative to heroic materialism, and that is not enough."[81] British historian Hugh Thomas writes of "the crisis which appears to affect the world in the last quarter of the twentieth century." He particularly worries that "half the population of the West itself seem sometimes to have lost faith in their own ideals."[82] James Billington warns that at a time when college students on leading American campuses regard Nietzsche as more important than Jeremiah or Saint Paul, "we are indeed in cultural crisis."[83]

Some less prominent scholars specifically interpret the retreat from marriage and family life as a portent of cultural crisis. Even a demographer such as Kingsley Davis can feel apocalyptic tremors as he contemplates marital and family trends which could mean (in his view) that "industrial societies will not survive."[84] Similarly, sociologist William Catton, Jr. sees the social acceptance of "ephemeral pairings" as an acceptable substitute for marriage as a development that "threatens societal viability — or even the persistence of human life itself."[85] Psychiatrist Boris Segal believes that "the disappearance of the religious foundations of marriage" is part of a "crisis of our culture" manifest in "disillusionment in religious and secular ideologies; decline of the intellectual authority of the Church and loss of unity with God; the disappearance of old taboos and restrictions; the loss of a sense of continuity and belonging."[86]

Many Americans still regard talk of a cultural crisis as overblown and premature. Others believe that marriage and family life can be culturally reaffirmed without a renascence of religion. Still others believe that a broad religious renewal can occur without a cultural cataclysm. My own assessment is that the United States is headed for unprecedented cultural and social trauma which may catalyze a renewed social commitment to marriage and family life. During the years and perhaps decades during which Americans do forestall catastrophe through managerial finesse, successful marriage will be neither rare nor normative, but will probably become increasingly difficult because of countervailing pressures. It may yet be some time before wedlock becomes a matter of love in the ruins, but no one will get rich in the years ahead by building wedding chapels.

— Bryce J. Christensen is director of The Rockford Institute Center on the Family in America.

ENDNOTES

[1] *Walker Percy,* Love in the Ruins: The Adventures of a Bad Catholic at a Time Near the End of the World *(New York: Farrar, Straus and Giroux, 1971).*

[2] *See Gene Brody, Eileen Beubaum, and Rex Forehand, "Serial Marriage: A Heuristic Analysis of an Emerging Family Form,"* Psychological Bulletin *103 (1988): 211-222.*

[3] *See Laurence L. Santi, "The Demographic Context of Recent Change in the Structure of American Households,"* Demography *25 (1988): 509-519; U.S. Bureau of the Census,* Statistical Abstract of the United States: 1988, 108th ed. *(Washington: U.S. Government Printing Office, 1987), p. 42.*

[4]See Andree Brooks, "Experts Find Extramarital Affairs Have a Profound Impact on Children," The New York Times, 9 March 1989, p. B16.

[5]Vern Bullough and Bonnie Bullough, Women and Prostitution: A Social History (Buffalo: Prometheus, 1987), p. 291.

[6]U.S. Bureau of the Census, Statistical Abstract of the United States: 1988, p. 83.

[7]Robert Schoen, "The Continuing Retreat From Marriage Figures From 1983, U.S. Marital Status Life Tables," Sociology and Social Research 71 (1987): 108-109.

[8]Thomas J. Espenshade, "The Recent Decline of American Marriage: Blacks and Whites in Comparative Perspective," in Contemporary Marriage: Comparative Perspectives on a Changing Institution, ed. Kingsley, Davis (New York: Russell Sage Foundation, 1985), p. 53.

[9]Kingsley Davis, "The Future of Marriage," in Contemporary Marriage, p. 32.

[10]Barbara F. Wilson and Kathryn A. London, "Going to the Chapel," American Demographics, December 1987, p. 29.

[11]Henry Sumner Maine, Ancient Law: Its Connection with the Early History of Society and Its Relation to Modern Ideas (1861; rpt. Gloucester, MA: Peter Smith, 1970), pp. 163-165.

[12]Kingsley Davis, "The Meaning and Significance of Marriage in Contemporary Society," in Contemporary Marriage, p. 19.

[13]See Susan Cotts Watkins et al., "Demographic Foundations of Family Change," American Sociological Review 52 (1987): 346-354.

[14]See Allan Carlson, "Family Breakdown and Other Cancers of the 'Post-Capitalist' Era," Persuasion at Work 6 (October 1983): 2-3.

[15]Allan Sherman, The Rape of the A*P*E (American * Puritan * Ethic): The Official History of the Sex Revolution (Chicago: Playboy Press, 1973), pp. 11, 338-339.

[16]See "'A Bunny's Tale': Christie Hefner Thinks It's a Bust" [interview], Chicago Tribune, 25 February 1985, Sec. 4, pp. 1, 7.

[17]Judith A. Reisman, "Content Analysis of Children, Crime and Violence in Playboy, Penthouse, and Hustler," Office of Juvenile Justice and Delinquency Prevention (OJJDP), Project No. 84-JN-AX-K007; telephone interview with Dr. Reisman, 30 November 1987.

[18]See Edward Donnerstein et al., The Question of Pornography: Research Findings and Policy Implications (New York: The Free Press, 1987), pp. 149-152.

[19]See United States Department of Justice, Attorney General's Commission on Pornography Final Report, July 1986 (Washington: U.S. Government Printing Office, 1986).

[20]See Allan Carlson, "Children in Poverty and Other Legacies of the Redistributive State," Persuasion at Work 10 (January 1987): 2.

[21]See Eugene Steurele, "The Tax Treatment of Households of Different Size," in Taxing the Family, ed. Rudolph G. Penner (Washington: American Enterprise Institute, 1983), p. 75.

[22]For a discussion of the antinatal effects of Social Security, see Charles F. Hohm et al., "A Reappraisal of the Social Security-Fertility Hypothesis: A Bidirectional Approach," The Social Science Journal 23 (1986): 149-168.

[23]Charles Murray, Losing Ground: American Social Policy, 1950-1980 (New York: Basic, 1984), pp. 154-162.

[24]Randal D. Day and Wade C. Mackey, "Children as Resources: A Cultural Analysis," Family Perspective 20 (1986): 258-262.

[25]*See Espenshade, "The Recent Decline of American Marriage," p. 77.*

[26]*Marian Wright Edelman,* Families in Peril: An Agenda for Social Change *(Cambridge: Harvard University Press, 1987), p. 72.*

[27]*David Popenoe,* Disturbing the Nest: Family Change and Decline in Modern Societies *(New York: Aldine de Gruyter, 1988), pp. 168-182, 237-239.*

[28]*Allan Carlson, "Toward 'The Working Family': The Hidden Agenda Behind the Comparable Worth Debate,"* Persuasion at Work *7 (July 1984): p. 4.*

[29]*See Hugh Thomas,* A History of the World *(New York: Harper & Row, 1979), p. 407.*

[30]*See Carolyn M. Newberger* et al., "The American Family in Crisis: Implications for Children," *Current Problems in Pediatrics 16 (1986): pp. 686-688.*

[31]*Lenore Weitzman, "The Divorce Law Revolution and the Transformation of Legal Marriage," in* Contemporary Marriage, *pp. 305, 335.*

[32]*Jack Douglas, "Pro-Family Laws Can Help Revitalize Family Life," unpublished* MS., *excerpted in the New Research section of* The Family in America *1 (April 1987): p. 1.*

[33]*Schoen, "The Continuing Retreat From Marriage," pp. 108-109.*

[34]*Betty Friedan,* The Feminine Mystique *(New York: W.W. Norton & Company, 1963), p. 176.*

[35]*Germaine Greer,* The Female Eunuch *(New York: McGraw Hill, 1971), pp. 216-220.*

[36]*Andrea Dworkin,* Our Blood: Prophecies and Discourses on Sexual Politics *(New York: Harper & Row, 1976), pp. 32, 82.*

[37]*Susan Brownmiller,* Against Our Will: Men, Women and Rape *(New York: Simon and Schuster, 1975), p. 376.*

[38]*Davis, "The Future of Marriage," p. 47.*

[39]*Gary Becker,* A Treatise on the Family *(Cambridge: Harvard University Press, 1981), p. 248.*

[40]*Robert S. McElvaine,* The End of the Conservative Era: Liberalism After Reagan *(New York: Arbor House, 1987), p. 100.*

[41]*Associated Press, "Young Men's Earnings Fall by Nearly One-Third,"* Rockford Register Star, *12 June 1987, p. 6A.*

[42]*Paul C. Matthiessen, "Changing Fertility and Family Formation in Denmark,"* World Health Statistics Quarterly *40 (1987): p. 64.*

[43]*See Plato,* The Republic, *V, in* Plato, *trans. B. Jowett, ed. Louise R. Loomis (Roslyn, NY: Walter J. Black, 1942), pp. 333-343; Thomas Campanella,* City of the Sun *(1623), trans. Thomas W. Halliday, in* Ideal Commonwealths, *rev. ed. (Port Washington, NY: Kennikat, 1968).*

[44]*Campanella,* City of the Sun, *pp. 147-148.*

[45]*B.F. Skinner,* Walden Two *(1948: rpt. New York: Macmillan, 1976), p. 126.*

[46]*H.G. Wells,* A Modern Utopia *(1905; rpt. Lincoln, NE: University of Nebraska Press, 1967), pp. 196, 200.*

[47]*William Morris,* News From Nowhere: Or an Epoch of Rest *(Boston: Roberts Brothers, 1891), pp. 78-79, 112-113.*

[48]*Edward Bellamy,* Looking Backward: 2000-1887 *(1888; rpt. New York: Random House, 1951), p. 214.*

[49]*See Becky L. Glass and Margaret K. Stolee, "Family Law in Soviet Russia, 1917-1945,"* Journal of Marriage and the Family *49 (1987): 893-901.*

[50]*Yevgeny Zamyatin,* We, *trans. Mirra Ginsburg (New York: Viking, 1972), pp. 20-21.*

[51]*Aldous Huxley, Intro. to* Brave New World *(1932; rpt. New York: Harper & Row, 1969), p. xiii.*

[52]*Huxley,* Brave New World, *pp. 128-132, 162-165.*

[53]*Huxley, Intro to* Brave New World, *pp. xiii, xiv.*

[54]*See Glass and Stolee, "Family Law in Soviet Russia, 1917-1945," pp. 898-901.*

[55]*See, for example, Sheila B. Kamerman, "Child Care Services: An Issue for Gender Equity and Women's Solidarity,"* Child Welfare *64 (1985): 262-264.*

[56]*Popenoe,* Disturbing the Nest, *p. 226.*

[57]*See Gallup international surveys for 1981 and 1968, Appendix in* Unsecular America, *ed. Richard John Neuhaus (Grand Rapids: William B. Eerdmans, 1986), pp. 115-127.*

[58]*See T.R. Balakrishnan et al., "A Hazard Model Analysis of the Covariates of Marriage Dissolution in Canada,"* Demography *24 (1987): 398-400; Allan F. Abrahamse et al.,* Beyond Stereotypes: Who Becomes a Single Teenage Mother? *(Santa Monica, CA: RAND Corporation, 1988), pp. 37-50; Mary Y. Morgan and John Scanzoni, "Religious Orientations and Women's Expected Continuity in the Labor Force,"* Journal of Marriage and the Family *49 (1987): 367-79.*

[59]*Bradley R. Hertel and Michael Hughes, "Religious Affiliation, Attendance, and Support for 'Pro-Family' Issues in the United States,"* Social Forces *65 (1987): 858-882.*

[60]*James H. Billington, "Education and Culture: Beyond 'Lifestyles,'" in* Virtue — Public and Private, *ed. Richard John Neuhaus (Grand Rapids: William B. Eerdmans, 1986), p. 4; see also "Explaining Virtue: A Report on a Conversation," in the same volume, pp. 54-55.*

[61]*Paul C. Vitz,* Censorship: Evidence of Bias in Our Children's Textbooks *(Ann Arbor: Servant, 1986), pp. 37-38.*

[62]*Peter Medawar,* The Limits of Science *(1984; rpt. New York: Oxford University Press, 1987), p. 35.*

[63]*John Milton,* Paradise Lost, *XII, 11, 648-649, in* John Milton: Complete Poems and Major Prose *(Indianapolis: Odyssey, 1957), p. 469.*

[64]*Zamyatin,* We, *p. 55.*

[65]*Skinner,* Walden Two, *pp. 279-281.*

[66]*Huxley,* Brave New World, *p. 163.*

[67]*Herbert Marcuse,* Eros and Civilization: A Philosophical Inquiry into Freud *(Boston: Beacon, 1955), pp. 201, 236-237.*

[68]*See, for instance, Nathan Glazer,* The Limits of Social Policy *(Cambridge: Harvard University Press, 1988), pp. 15-25; Charles R. Morris,* A Time of Passion: America, 1960-1980 *(New York: Harper & Row, 1984), pp. 180-181, 190-191, 222-24.*

[69]*Stephen Chapman, "RX for dying babies: Better mothers, not more money,"* Chicago Tribune, *14 August 1988, Sec. 4, p. 3.*

[70]*Terry Arendell,* Mothers and Divorce: Legal, Economic and Social Dilemmas *(Berkeley: University of California Press, 1986), p. 160.*

[71]*Christopher Jencks, "Deadly Neighborhoods," rev. of* The Truly Disadvantaged: The Inner City, The Underclass, and Public Policy, *by William Julius Wilson,* The New Republic, *13 June 1988, pp. 27-30.*

[72]*Randal D. Day and Wade C. Mackey, "The Mother-State-Child 'Family': Cul-de-Sac or Path to the Future?"* The Family in America *2 (March 1988): 6.*

[73]*Robert Schoen and James R. Kluegel, "The Widening Gap in Black and White*

Marriage Rates: The Impact of Population Composition and Differential Marriage Propensities," American Sociological Review *53 (1968): 895-907.*

[74]*Martin Plissner, "The Marriage Gap,"* Public Opinion, *February/March 1987, p. 53.*

[75]*Ida Sasser, "Political Activity Among Working-Class Women in a U.S. City,"* American Ethnologist *13 (1986): 108.*

[76]*Alice Rossi, "Beyond the Gender Gap: Women's Bid for Political Power,"* Social Science Quarterly *64 (1983): 726-727.*

[77]*See Neil Gilbert, "Sweden's Disturbing Family Trends,"* The Wall Street Journal, *24 June 1987, p. 27.*

[78]*Popenoe,* Disturbing the Nest, *p. 305.*

[79]*Pitirim Sorokin,* Social and Cultural Dynamics: Ethics, Law, and Social Relationships, *abridged ed. (1957; rpt. New Brunswick: Transaction Books, 1985), pp. 700-702.*

[80]*Aleksandr I. Solzhenitsyn,* A World Split Apart: Commencement Address Delivered at Harvard University, June 8, 1978, *trans. Irina Ilovayskaya Alberti (New York: Harper & Row, 1978), pp. 51, 57.*

[81]*Kenneth Clark,* Civilisation: A Personal View *(New York: Harper & Row, 1969), pp. 346-347.*

[82]*Thomas,* A History of the World, *p. 616.*

[83]*See "Exploring Virtue: A Report on Conversation," in* Virtue — Public and Private, *pp. 54-55.*

[84]*Davis, "The Meaning and Significance of Marriage," pp. 19-20.*

[85]*William R. Catton, Jr., "Family 'Divorce Heritage' and Its Intergenerational Transmission: Toward a System-Level Perspective,"* Sociological Perspectives *31 (1988): 416-417.*

[86]*Boris M. Segal, "A Borderline Style of Functioning — the Role of Family, Society and Heredity: An Overview,"* Child Psychiatry and Human Development *18 (1988): 226, 230.*

Participants in "The Retreat From Marriage" Conference

May 11-12, 1989

Chairman

Allan C. Carlson
President of The Rockford Institute
Rockford, Illinois

Authors of Papers

Herbert L. Smith
Assistant professor at the Population Studies Center
University of Pennsylvania
Philadelphia, PA

Norval D. Glenn
Ashbel Smith professor of sociology at the University of Texas
Austin, TX

Jack Douglas
Professor of sociology at the University of California-San Diego
La Jolla, CA

Bryce J. Christensen
Director of The Rockford Institute Center on the Family in
America
Rockford, IL

Other Participants

Nabers Cabaniss
Deputy assistant secretary for population affairs
Department of Health and Human Services
Washington, D.C.

Randal Day
Associate professor of child and family studies
Washington State University
Pullman, WA

Thomas Fleming
Editor of Chronicles: A Magazine of American Culture
Rockford, IL

Jacqueline Kasun
Professor of economics at the Humboldt State University
Arcata, CA

William Mattox
Policy analyst, Family Research Council
Washington, D.C.

Richard Neely
Justice of the West Virginia Supreme Court of Appeals
Charleston, WV

Steven Nock
Associate professor of sociology at the University of Virginia
Charlottesville, VA

David Popenoe
Professor of sociology at Rutgers State University
New Brunswick, NJ

Robert Schoen
Professor of sociology at the University of Illinois
Urbana, IL

Maris Vinovskis
Professor of history at Michigan University
Ann Arbor, MI

Paul Vitz
Professor of psychology at the New York University
New York, NY

'The Retreat From Marriage': Summary of a Discussion

Fourteen people — drawn from various backgrounds in the social sciences and from the world of public policy — gathered in May 1989 at The Rockford Inn in Rockford, Illinois, to consider "The Retreat From Marriage." The four papers published in this volume framed the central questions, but the discussion among participants engaged many other cultural and social topics.

Opening the discussion, chairman Allan Carlson focused participants' attention on the major issues for consideration. He explained that "The Retreat From Marriage" entailed changes in the meaning of marriage in recent decades. He urged participants to explore why these changes are happening, what their future consequences will be, and what — if anything — should be done about them. The examination of such questions should extend beyond the American context, since a similar and perhaps even accelerated movement away from marriage may be discerned in other countries throughout the Western World, notably in Sweden.

In presenting his paper, Herbert Smith described the growth in the number of nonmarital births since World War II as "a fairly smooth exponential curve." He stressed that since overall fertility has been falling in the United States, "the proportion of all births that are nonmarital has gone up drastically." Such trends mean that illegitimacy will have different consequences — and different meanings — for different generations.

In assessing the difference between races in nonmarital fertility, he thought it important to remember that premarital pregnancies among whites are far more likely to be legitimated by marriage than are premarital pregnancies among blacks. However, the widespread notion that illegitimacy is a problem peculiar to minority populations — specifically blacks — will not bear close scrutiny. Since 1980, more white children have been born out of wedlock than black children. The rates of nonmarital fertility among whites are now as high as they have ever been. On the other hand, nonmarital fertility rates have not changed very much among the nonwhite population, and are lower in the 1980's than they were twenty years earlier.

Smith pointed out that this downward trend in nonmarital fertility began before the *Roe* v. *Wade* decision of 1973, which legalized abortion. He speculated that perhaps the downturn was the consequence of economic progress for blacks. Contraceptives proliferated during the era in question, but use of contraceptives is more important for explaining white fertility than black. When Smith shifted attention from illegitimacy rates to illegitimacy ratios, he discerned a quite different pattern. Unlike the illegitimacy rate (the number of nonmarital births per 1,000 women), the illegitimacy ratio gives the proportion of all children who are born out of wedlock. Within the black population, the illegitimacy ratio has long since passed the 50 percent mark. Clearly, the social functions of legitimacy and the stigmatization of illegitimacy have broken down among blacks. With white illegitimacy ratios now at the level of nonwhite illegitimacy ratios around 1940, the question is how far white fertility is likely to travel on the same road trod by nonwhites during the past half century. Smith noted that the rising illegitimacy ratios do not — at least among blacks — reflect rising illegitimacy rates. Rather, among both blacks and whites, fewer couples are marrying, marriages come later, more marriages end in divorce or separation, and fertility has dropped within marriage. These shifts toward nonmarital fertility must be taken into account in thinking about the future composition of school systems, day-care programs, and the workforce.

Turning to divorce rates, Smith described a pattern of logistic curves in recent decades, as rates rose sharply from a previously stable level, but now seem to have reached a plateau. Still, Smith expressed skepticism about the apparent leveling off of the divorce rate. He conjectured that if the age of marrying couples were fully taken into account, the divorce rate might still be climbing. Smith underscored the number of children involved in divorces in recent decades. He resisted the notion that remarriage completely mitigates the effects of divorce upon a child. Although a number of studies have shown that having children reduces the likelihood of divorce, he mentioned evidence that children now provide less protection against divorce than in the past.

Among couples married in recent years, fully half will be divorced during their lifetime. Some researchers report that perhaps up to two-thirds may be headed for divorce, although Smith harbored some suspicion about the manner in which this higher fraction was calculated. He cited a recent article finding that for marriages contracted in the late 70's and early 80's, the level of divorce within five years has held fairly steady at 22-23 percent. Complaining that divorce statistics are often misinterpreted, Smith underscored the distinction between the divorce rate for marriages formed in any year and the divorce rate for all marriages in existence. Since divorce rates are highest during the first seven years of marriage but the average extant marriage is already of longer duration, the divorce rate of all marriages in existence runs much lower than 50 percent. At any point in time, about one existing marriage in five will end in divorce, but of all marriages contracted in any given year at least half will terminate in divorce.

In concluding his oral presentation, Smith discounted the widely held belief that "values are driving the process" of escalating divorce. Other social and economic forces are at play, he suggested.

Serving as discussant for Professor Smith's paper, Robert Schoen praised Smith for his analysis, identifying as particularly useful the discussion of the difference between nonmarital fertility rates and nonmarital fertility ratios. While Schoen felt that rates usually capture changes in behavior over time, he conceded that for nonmarital fertility, rates may not provide the best measure. He noted that the advantages of looking at nonmarital ratios rather than rates appear particularly clear when considering the black community, where nonmarital fertility has leveled off and even declined, but the proportion of all black children born out of wedlock has risen sharply. The reason that approximately 60 percent of black births are out of wedlock is that so many young black women do not marry until relatively late or do not marry at all.

Since women who are not married are at risk of bearing a child out of wedlock, changes in the marriage rate determine the number at risk. Schoen reported that among women born in 1930 about 97 percent of those who survived to age 15 eventually married. For women born in 1950, the comparable figure is 95 percent. In 1983 — the latest year for which figures are available — the proportion dropped to 90 percent. Age at marriage has also risen. For women born in 1930, the average age of marriage is just over 21; for those born in 1950, the average age stands at just under 22. The average age for women marrying in 1983 was 24.5 — showing a rather substantial rise in a measure that tends not to change very much. Schoen saw evidence in the statistics that the retreat from marriage has been going on for a considerable time. The rise in divorce may also be traced back at least to the late 19th century. For women born in 1920, the chance of marriage ending in divorce stood at 29 percent. For those born in 1950, the figure stood at 42 percent. For marriages formed in 1983, the projected likelihood of divorce is 44 percent. The overall pattern constitutes a remarkably linear increase in the proportion of marriages ending in divorce. Not only does the rising risk of divorce have a long history in this country, but similar long-term patterns may be seen in other countries such as Sweden, Belgium, England, and Wales.

Schoen argued that the apparent plateau in the divorce level must be interpreted in light of the rise in cohabitation, which has artificially reduced the number of couples at risk for divorce. Many unions are formed, he remarked, that perhaps in the past would have been marriages. When cohabiting unions dissolve neither the formation nor the dissolution of the unions enter into the statistics, making divorce rates appear deceptively low.

In the rise in cohabitation, Schoen saw "the most serious threat to marriage as an institution. Out-of-wedlock births can be legitimated; divorces can be just the replacement of one marital partner by another; cohabitation substitutes a different institutional form for marriage." Schoen characterized cohabitation as substantively different from marriage, as a "looser and less permanent union, one where there is more interdependence between the partners, one where the partners hold lower expectations for one another."

Schoen joined Smith in cautioning against an emphasis on changing values as the cause of the retreat from marriage. Not that values have not changed, but that the retreat from marriage probably reflects changes in the American economy and in the role of women in the economy. Cohabitation, for instance, is an institutional form that is particularly well-fit for two-earner, no-children households. As the economy has changed, the shifting trade between males and females has helped shape different social and family relationships. Working women now have more alternatives to an unsatisfactory marriage than do unemployed women. The employment of wives creates new alternatives for husbands as well. If a wife's employment gives her greater control over the marriage, husbands may devalue the relationship, making it a consensual union rather than a true marriage.

Opening the general discussion, David Popenoe drew attention to the divergent possible meanings of nonmarital fertility. He outlined the varying possible consequences for a birth outside of marriage. Among blacks in the United States, the overwhelming majority of babies born out of wedlock will grow up without a father. However, in Iceland where 52 percent of all births occur outside marriage, unmarried parents typically marry a few months or a year after the birth of their child, and a large number of these couples remain married. Because of this pattern, Popenoe judged Iceland's illegitimacy ratio of 52 percent as "not terribly significant." In Sweden, a country with a nonmarital birth rate about as high as Iceland's, couples are much less likely to marry than they are in Iceland, but they often live together out of wedlock for a lifetime. On the other hand, many Swedish cohabiting couples do break up. In any case, Popenoe hoped that other participants would look beyond simply the nonmarital birth rate to consider the social consequences of nonmarital birth.

Amplifying this concern, Maris Vinovskis wondered whether concern should be focused on the retreat from marriage or on the retreat from dual parenthood. Historically, he noted that fairly large proportions of Western European and American women had not married in the 19th century. In part because no married woman could pursue a career, about a fifth of women in Massachusetts in 1870 never married. Many women also delayed marriage until their mid 20's. Such patterns are not unusual, nor did Vinovskis find them troubling. But when women who do not marry do bear children, then the retreat from marriage becomes more problematic — at least from the children's point of view.

Steven Nock expressed puzzlement over the fact that 60 percent of black children are born out of wedlock, yet an estimated 90 percent of American women will marry, but Smith and Schoen collaborated to explain that although only about 20 percent of blacks will never marry, black women typically marry after childbearing. A black woman may well bear a child in her teens yet not marry until her late 20's. In his reading of recent research, Smith did not see black stepfathers significantly mitigating the consequences of illegitimate birth for their stepchildren.

Directing his question to Vinovskis, Randal Day wondered whether single parents had not been fairly common in the 19th century because of accidents and disease. In the broad historical sweep, how common has it been for a child to be reared by two parents?

Vinovskis responded that death often did break up families in the past, citing particularly high death rates in the Chesapeake Bay area during the 17th and 18th centuries. The unprecedented carnage of the Civil War also disrupted many families. In common usage, "the family" refers to an idealized 19th-century family which was not always typical of the 19th century. "As we measure ourselves against the past," he ventured, "we should not do it against an idealized past." "Children have always lived with uncertainty," he further remarked. Yet Vinovskis believed it was a mistake to equate widows with the parents of illegitimate children. Widows are perceived and treated differently than never-married parents.

Reinforcing a theme raised by Vinovskis, Day urged all participants to "guard against the idea of the classical family of Western nostalgia." Conceding that while attitudes toward divorce and the children of divorce had shifted, he doubted whether "the Waltons ever really existed."

Bryce Christensen saw things differently, pointing out that even when marriage was often disrupted by death in the 19th century, the commitment to marital permanence as a moral ideal was still very strong in a way that it is not today. Christensen dissented from the view that divorce has simply replaced death as the way marriages terminate. While it is possible to make a statistical case for such a view up until 1960, since that time the rise in the divorce rate has far outstripped the fall in rates for widowhood.

Vinovskis took this as an opening to disagree with Schoen and Smith about the importance of culture and attitudes in determining marital behavior. He noted that if people living in the 19th century had been "lucky enough to have an economist or sociologist to talk with them, they would have divorced or wouldn't have married in the first place. People held marriages together, had children under very adverse circumstances." In the past, people often held marriages together that were "economically inefficient." People living in the 1830's and 1840's — a time when poverty was very widespread — still accepted marriage as an ideal and attempted to achieve it. Vinovskis found it very unfortunate that many arguments about culture look only at developments since

World War II or since the 1960's. In a broader historical analysis, culture plays a much more important role and deserves more attention than short-term studies would suggest.

Popenoe thought it remarkable that we are the first civilization in history in which a child is often raised by one person in a private room or dwelling. Despite the relatively high mortality of parents, children in the past were surrounded by adults responsible for their care.

Reverting to the question of single parenting, Nock pointed out that no matter what measure is used — employment, income, prestige — children raised their first six years in single-parent families end up with much lower levels of adult attainment than do children reared by two parents. These effects cannot be explained by household income, race, or age at divorce, nor do they appear any different for the children of divorce than for illegitimate children. The handicap of being reared in a single-parent household during early years appears widespread and persistent.

Before discussion proceeded further along that line, Allan Carlson asked those present to address "the question of values," briefly touched on by Smith and Schoen, both of whom had asserted that changes in values had reflected rather than caused changes in marital behavior. For Carlson, the issue of values defined "an important philosophical question."

Not to be misunderstood, Smith acknowledged "large-scale, long-term cultural changes" in family life. Yet he remained pessimistic about the possibility of finding anything in a few decades of attitudinal change that would somehow provide "a lever on the situation." Recalling the experience of a colleague whose son brought home a school book about a boy spending time with his divorced father, Smith felt that Americans must either face the reality of a growing number of children touched by divorce, or they must "go around putting scarlet letters on kids." The case is not that values are not important, Smith concluded, but rather that it is difficult to tell whether values determine social behavior or vice versa.

Richard Neely appealed for an historical understanding of values, cautioning against an assessment of "values in the abstract." Noting that all of Smith's charts had gone back only to 1940, the year before his birth, Neely observed that "the way the world has changed within my lifetime is overwhelming." He recalled that during his childhood some people still plowed with horses. His own grandmother spent the first 20 years of life in the world before automobiles, while the father of his immediate predecessor in the West Virginia Supreme Court had fought with Stonewall Jackson in the Shenandoah Valley in the War between the States. In sum, "the world has changed more since 1941 than it changed between the time Tiberius became emperor until 1940. A Roman in heartland America in 1936 would have been a great deal more at home than an American who died in 1900 and was resurrected in 1989."

Neely identified the employment of women as one of the most striking changes during the last five decades. In 1940, when coal was mined with a pick and a shovel and a little dynamite and when other American businesses imposed similar physical demands, there was no paid work for women. In the past, women did work — and worked hard — on farms, but employment opportunities for women have opened up in an age of computers and information processing, while the demand for a man's strong back has disappeared. While disputing the assertion (found in Christensen's paper) that the movement of women into the labor force has eroded a man's ability to earn a family wage — an erosion he attributed to international competition and the decline of the unions — he did believe that the shift in employment opportunities for men and women had wrought a profound value change in family life. In many modern situations — including his own judicial office — Neely noted an employment bias favoring women over men, because of their higher tolerance for dull, monotonous work. "How," he asked, "would a 19th-century family respond to job opportunities where there was actually a preference given for women?"

The word *value* made Thomas Fleming uneasy, since it connotes a marketplace image, a market in which people "trade" values in the way they trade money, prestige, goods, or efforts. On the other hand, *values* sometimes refer to "something like tradition or the way we do things: what the Romans called *mos maiorum*, the habits of our ancestors." In still a different usage, *values* refers to the religious or philosophical convictions of people who believe that their pattern of living actually reflects not merely inherited social conventions, but rather the way the universe is constructed or (more commonly) the way God has commanded them to live. Religious convictions of this sort are far from "values" available for bartering in the marketplace. Indeed, Fleming judged the phrase "religious value" to be a contradiction in terms.

Engaging the specific issue of female employment, Fleming was not at all sure that recent changes were independent of "so-called values." The movement of women into the workforce is not independent of religious conviction, not independent of inherited ancestral traditions, not independent of philosophic changes in the understanding of the relationship between the sexes, and certainly not independent of legal changes governing relations between men and women, husband and wife, and parent and child. In any case, Fleming warned that any discussion of "values" would lead to a dead end without precise specification of the meaning of the term.

Smith accepted the need to define values, but he begged to differ with Fleming's characterization of female labor. After all, he argued, women have worked in agrarian societies. The period during which women stayed at home while men went out to work was relatively short.

In Neely's opinion, technology has also changed the amount of time that a woman can actually devote to home. In the past, a woman on the farm could combine her responsibilities for child care with various other essential tasks. Those tasks are now largely gone because of the complete segregation of the home and the workplace. Even cooking now involves no preparation of raw materials. Because of these changes, Neely reported that without young children even a traditional woman (like his own wife) would go crazy staying at home.

Disagreements over definitions aside, Jack Douglas marveled at the "sea change" in the American experience in family life. He conceded the persistence in past eras of an underclass in which illegitimacy and cohabitation were common; yet, he was astounded at the current prevalence of divorce and cohabitation among the affluent and well educated. Such things are no longer regarded as shameful or embarrassing by many upper-class Americans. Citing Paul Vitz's work, Douglas noted how school textbooks mirror this movement away from family norms by the nation's cultural elite. Even official statistics understate the magnitude of the shift. Douglas conjectured that in suburban California the "emotional divorce rate" might run 150 percent, since couples who divorce typically pass through a couple attempts at cohabitation as well. Douglas also lamented the decline of the sense of duty which in the past prompted grandparents, aunts, and uncles to take over the rearing of children when the nuclear family broke down. Douglas could see few of these extended family relationships at work in areas — especially black slums — now supported by the government.

Christensen drew a distinction between popular attitudes and the world views of cultural elites. Popular attitudes, he opined, often simply reflect the way the economy happens to be structured. However, Christensen strenuously objected to a Marxian analysis that describes moral orientation as simply "the smoke above the economic fire." He dismissed this kind of analysis as deeply dehumanizing. Instead, he affirmed the decisive long-term importance of the convictions held by the cultural elite. As an example of a significant change in such conviction, he noted the emergence for the first time in 19th-century and early 20th-century America of atheism as an intellectually respected outlook. Underscoring the importance of such changes, he protested that if all intellectual conviction is simply a matter of economic circumstance, then the life of the mind — including this very conference — is no more than a play of shadows, a charade, and a sham.

From a different perspective, Smith noted the frequency with which people adhere to traditional values, while still practicing nontraditional behaviors. Carlson wanted to label this behavior as hypocrisy, but Smith thought it simply a matter of people finding themselves in circumstances beyond their control. While he did not dismiss the importance of people's belief, he nonetheless suggested that belief is not an independent engine that always drives human behavior.

Vinovskis remarked that his own version of the 19th century — especially female labor during that period — differed from some versions advanced by other participants. More fundamentally, he complained that scholars feel uncomfortable in discussions of values, because they do not devote the time and attention to them that they should. From his perspective, the rise of individualism counted as one of the major changes in American history in the 19th century, resulting in an increasing unwillingness over time to take responsibility for one's own actions or those of others. Vinovskis believed that this trend has intensified since World War II, as fewer people have shown themselves willing to intrude in the lives of others to impose a moral sanction. Is it possible to redesign society in such a way that people — especially males — will continue to accept the responsibilities of marriage when all negative sanctions have been abandoned? Because of the importance of this question, Vinovskis dismissed "values" surveys which do not determine the willingness of those who respond to impose negative sanctions.

Paul Vitz returned to the relationship between values and social circumstances. He found it intriguing that in surveys of opinion toward female employment, husbands' attitudes seemed to reflect whatever their wives were doing. If a husband's attitude changed, it usually changed after — not before — his wife went to work. This evidence suggests that when their daily realities change, people will reassess some of their less fundamental beliefs.

Concurring in this analysis, Norval Glenn thought it a mistake to suppose that changes in family life are governed by values alone or economics alone. The interaction between the two is complex, he said.

Fleming invoked a literary reflection on the contrast between the way people live and what they believe. He recalled Julia Peterkin's famous novel *Scarlet Sister Mary* about a black woman who is expelled from her church in South Carolina because she is seduced by a glamorous young man. She lives in sin, bears children out of wedlock, marries, and then sees her marriage fall apart. Despite her love for the man who seduces her and for her children, she has a conviction of sin and guilt and acknowledges herself as Scarlet Sister Mary. By the end of the book, she has changed her life substantially, has brought her life back into accord with her ideals, and is finally reaccepted by the church congregation. Fleming took the book as an illustration of how conflicts between conduct and belief can be eventually resolved so long as the ideal is consistently upheld by the church community.

Looking at historical trends beginning long before World War II, Christensen pointed to the emergence of a money economy as a cultural development that has powerfully affected family life. Before the 18th-century, he observed, most people did not think of getting ahead. Rather, they labored for subsistence, getting through. Christensen conjectured that while the "getting-ahead mentality" fosters individualism, the "getting-through mentality" proves more conducive to community interest and to family life. This shift in mentality is deeper and more fundamental than most issues normally included under the rubric of "values." Christensen further posited a link between this shift and another change in the way people live and make decisions. Describing calculation as a mode of thought that is memory-killing, Christensen asserted that fewer people live by memory now, and more people live by calculation. This has caused a sort of "intergenerational amnesia." Relatively few people can now describe very much of the texture of their grandparents' lives.

Responding to Christensen's discussion of the money economy, Neely invoked Marx as an interpreter. Though contemptuous of Marxist economics, Neely credited Marx with a brilliant sociological insight in his notion that moral ideals are largely derived from the material basis of society. Yet what of religious values? Neely asked. He noted that all major religions — especially Christianity — are historical religions whose historical bases have been under fire at least since Copernicus. Among those educated at the nation's elite theology schools — at Berkeley or Yale, for instance — most clerics are almost secular humanists using religious poetry. As he surveyed American clergymen, Neely could see unqualified belief in the Resurrection only at "the level of the two-year associate degree Baptist preacher, somewhere in Bullsnort, West Virginia." In Neely's assessment, traditional values are in trouble because modern science has undermined the credibility of religion for the nation's cultural leadership.

Turning from religion to morality, Popenoe was intrigued by Vinovskis' comment on the decline of negative sanctions. He recalled Margaret Mead's observation that there has never been a society in which men stayed married to their wives for life unless culturally compelled to do so. We may be, he ventured, the first society which has taken away most of the compulsions. As a consequence, many children will reach adulthood without having lived continuously with both biological parents, a development likely to have profound effects.

It will probably spell the end of the culture, Vitz gloomily suggested. As a psychologist who sees clients with personal problems, he found that failed cohabitation imposes much the same harmful psychological effects as divorce, even though cohabitational divorces do not show up in any statistics.

Returning to one of Christensen's themes, Vitz reported evidence that the individualistic ethos of getting ahead may now be "wearing thin, not just conceptually and intellectually, but economically." A new gentry is developing, devoted to an ecology movement premised upon cultural maintenance, not cultural growth. A rustication of some kind is setting in as more Americans reject the getting and spending mentality and look for stability. Vitz interpreted this conference itself as part of the effort to regain stability.

Vitz urged those concerned about renewing negative sanctions to remember the positive benefits of long-term committed relationships between men and women. He found it regrettable that the positive notion of committed relationship was often omitted from our cultural calculus. He encouraged a shifting of emphasis away from the evils of not marrying to the depth and richness that comes through marriage.

Day attempted an anthropological evaluation of recent cultural patterns in family life. He asserted that the ideal family that Americans measure themselves against developed in a patriarchal agricultural society, even though most anthropologists would say that humanity has spent 99 percent of its existence as hunters and gatherers, with very low birth rates and with egalitarian relationships between the sexes.

Fleming contested Day's characterization of hunter-gatherer societies as sexually egalitarian. Such societies are perhaps more egalitarian than classical China or Greece, but men still control all the positions of prestige and status. Besides, tribes of hunters and gatherers have often been marginalized by more highly developed tribes.

Concurring, Day said that his point was precisely that as they send both husband and wife into the workplace and allow their fertility to drop below replacement level, modern Americans are adopting the unsuccessful cultural pattern of a hunter-gatherer people.

Speaking as an economist rather than anthropologist, Jacqueline Kasun confessed that she did not see such a great change in women's role in recent decades. Women have always worked, she affirmed, noting that all of her female ancestors were businesswomen, traders, and farm managers. As far back as the book of Proverbs in the Bible, Kasun noted, we find a picture of a woman who was an ingenious, energetic achiever, who does try to get ahead by buying a field and cultivating it (see Prov. 31). Meanwhile, her husband spends the day sitting in the gate looking important. Kasun dismissed that little woman who stayed behind the door a generation ago as a caricature that fails to correspond to any person in the real world.

Kasun drew her own insights into the relationship between morality and economics from her work with young women who had had abortions. Despite the preachments in favor of abortion by the cultural elite, these young women felt that abortion was wrong, but that their circumstances left them no choice. Kasun concluded from interviews with such young women that people do possess "some inner knowledge of values that is not determined by economic circumstances," even if those circumstances do sometimes make it difficult for people to live in harmony with those values. Kasun took encouragement from the evident failure of the nation's cultural elites to shape youthful attitudes to their social agenda.

When Smith wondered just who these mysterious elites are, Neely responded that America does not have one elite group, but rather four competing elites: the academic elite, the political elite, the business elite, and the media elite. The academic elite enjoy a lock on cultural pretension, but have no money, so they loathe and despise the business elite. The business elite understand that they are all basically Babbitts, but they have loads of money. They despise, detest, and loathe the academic elite, because of their cultural pretensions. The political elite are reasonably well off, but still they hate the business elite for being much richer. With less intensity, the political elite dislike the academic elite as "ankle biters" who point out their errors in scholarly journals. But the political elites' great nemesis is the media elite. The media elite believe that they are just as intelligent and cultivated as the academic elite, and they are outraged that they are not much more powerful than the business elite. Consequently, the media elite regularly attack the business and political elites.

The elite group in America most supportive of the family, Neely continued, is the business elite. The academic elite do not believe in the family, because they trade in novelty. The professor who writes an academic article saying the family is wonderful does not get tenure at Harvard. Rather, professors strain to come up with wild new theories they can publish. Because they are actually in the entertainment not the information business, the media elite like-wise largely ignores stable, happy families and focuses instead on the aberrant and sensational. Neely maintained that because of these conflicting strategies — not consciously designed by those who pursue them — the nation has no single elite, but rather several different elites fighting one another over status and power.

Fleming pointed out that in outlining his scheme of conflicting elites that Neely had violated classic elite theory of the sort developed by the Italian sociologists such as Mosca and Pareto. Though professing no personal adherence to this theory, Fleming explained that according to classical elite theory, a single governing class can be identified in any society as the group who set the tone for the whole of that society. As an admirable application of classical elite theory to American circumstances, Fleming cited James Burnham's *Managerial Revolution*, which argued almost 50 years ago that the capitalist business elite was being replaced by a new elite class of managers in the academy, in labor unions, in government, and in business. This succession of elites explains why top managers in business move so easily into government and back to a Harvard professional school and back into government. Because of the managerial revolution, the people at the very top in all sectors of society share a very similar mindset.

Vinovskis protested that the province of cultural leadership is a contested terrain in all cultural domains. He disputed Neeley's assertion that academics are opposed to the family because of their fascination with novelty, arguing that nowadays the professor who asserts that marriage might work would be saying the novel thing that would be easier to publish than the now-stale view that marriage is doomed to failure. In any case, Vinovskis could see no direct translation of the professoriat's work into community attitudes. Since leadership is contested in all segments of culture, each individual must decide upon a personal position for family issues.

Vinovskis was doubtful about Vitz' recommendation that marriage could be fostered by emphasizing its positive rewards. He feared that once people start doing cost-benefit analysis of marriage, they have already changed the nature of wedlock. A recovery of a sense of responsibility seemed essential, though Vinovskis admitted that responsibility is not a popular notion in contemporary society. Perhaps responsibility can be inculcated by focusing on the needs of the child. In calling for a renewed sense of responsibility, however, Vinovskis expressed nervousness about Jack Douglas' paper as exemplifying the kind of jeremiads now coming from conservatives who say the world is coming down. Although conceding that such views contain elements of truth,

Vinovskis complained that conservative rhetoric often smacks of conspiracy theory and is far removed from the reality he sees.

Exercising a chairman's prerogative, Carlson intervened to ask participants to consider Schoen's claim that cohabitation is a more serious challenge than divorce to marriage as an institution. Nock responded that the threat to marriage from cohabitation depends upon whether people cohabit as a prelude to marriage or as an alternative to marriage. Available evidence suggested to him that most Americans who cohabit do go on to marry, making cohabitation a part of courtship, not a replacement for marriage. Yet Nock worried about current social responses to cohabitation. He observed that in the past most forms of shame and most events which established reputation were associated with transitions in the family. In cases of illegitimacy or sexual misalliance, those involved might be publicly humiliated in a ritual of sorts such as the shivaree, a practice in pre-19th century Europe in which villagers would noisily surround the home of someone who had violated community standards. Now, however, personal reputation depends far less than in the past upon family transitions and behavior in violation of family norms such as cohabitation or adultery. Today, reputation is established with the credentials won by moving through educational programs or occupational opportunities.

Vinovskis' previous comment upon the need to renew a sense of responsibility prompted Christensen to ask, Responsibility to whom? Professing a personal belief that after death he would answer to his ancestors for his mortal conduct, Christensen conceded that belief in responsibility to ancestors has grown rare, a development that has recently worried British philosopher Mary Midgley. Christensen conjectured that young couples would probably not cohabit if they believe they must eventually give an account of their lives to departed grandparents, but that they might well choose to cohabit if they consider their grandparents irrelevant people, conveniently forgotten.

Invoking a less other-worldly reinforcement of family responsibility, Fleming emphasized the essential "mechanism of shame" operative in a face-to-face society in which everyone must maintain good relations with relatives and friends in order to obtain food, marry, and rear children. These mechanisms of shame no longer operate for modern individuals who can avoid the consequences of disgrace simply by moving from one city to another.

Sympathetic to the notion that there are too few negative sanctions for behaviors harmful to families and communities, Smith nonetheless resisted the idea that the past held something good which now we have lost. Smith doubted the objectivity of a group of white males in assessing "the good old days." How good were they? he questioned. Alluding to the horrors of the two world wars, he characterized the whole 20th century as a fundamental assault on 19th century assumptions and values. He traced the Holocaust and this century's murderous warfare in part to a misplaced trust in institutions governed by patriarchy. Smith saw no inconsistency between a belief in family and cultural responsibilities and his enjoyment at living in this century rather than an earlier one.

Fleming objected that the soldiers who have served in this century as concentration camp guards or as shock troops have been prepared for their tasks by political indoctrination which has deprived them of the sense of shame found in the face-to-face society of a traditional village. He did not persuade Smith.

Douglas lamented the historical amnesia of Americans, few of whom know what happened ten years ago, to say nothing of the 19th century. What now appears as a sea change in social attitudes toward behavior is actually the outcome of a long-term social drift. From a rate of less than one per 1,000 at the end of the last century, divorce has slowly but steadily grown in frequency and acceptance. Because this cultural trend is so deep, the divorce and abortion rates for a semi-Western city like Moscow run as high as those in Beverly Hills, the epitome of a very different society.

Among the American elite, Douglas sensed continuing pressure against the family from a "New Class" of academics, bureaucrats, media, and politicians, guided by a collective sense of self-interest and a generalized modernism. Douglas blamed the New Class for perpetuating a myth of Victorians as evil, hypocritical, and repressive people. Douglas complained that a modernist bias in journalism and publishing made it hard to challenge modernist views on the family.

Returning to the issue of reputation, William Mattox detected a breakdown in social consensus about what defines a good or bad reputation. He reasoned that perhaps we now tend to romanticize the past because — regardless of what problems people had then —

they did share a consensus about what families should do. He thought that the past consensus about family life sprang from a Judeo-Christian heritage, so that the erosion of religiosity has meant the loss of this consensus. As religion has faded — and with it the belief in a reconciliation for the penitent — Americans have grown hesitant about saying "This is good" or "This is bad," lest they impose guilt that cannot be redeemed in some way.

Interested but not convinced, Smith pointed to the fairly high level of religious feeling expressed in surveys by blacks who nonetheless continue to bear a high proportion of their children out of wedlock. Blacks living in the Philadelphia ghetto talk about the traditional family, but they don't live it. In contrast, Smith viewed his own traditional family life not as the result of religious belief — since he professed none — but as the consequence of favorable economic circumstances. The structure of the economy and the society, he argued, affects family life more than religious belief.

Carlson remarked that by statistical measures the United States is a very religious nation, since Americans attend church more than most other people; yet perhaps religious teaching now affects American behavior less than in the past. For Carlson, the American turn away from family life appeared especially striking in the marked decline in fertility, particularly within marriage, in the 1970's and 1980's.

Day worried that divorce and illegitimacy would be misinterpreted if regarded as end states rather than as adaptive transitions. Such transitions may not be viewed as ideal, since they do impose costs, but most of the people involved in divorce and illegitimacy do finally marry and stay married.

Smith partly corroborated Day's point, agreeing that most of those who divorce do remarry. Still, he stressed that second marriages are statistically less stable than first marriages and that third marriages are "like riding a motorcycle without a helmet."

In the final comment of the first session of the conference, Neely insisted on the distinction between the short-term cohabitation practiced by young people who are "just fiddlin' around" and the long-term cohabitation of older people whose unions are quite different.

As he summarized his paper to open the second session of the conference, Glenn conceded that the title of his paper — "The Social and Cultural Meaning of Contemporary Marriage" — was too pretentious for a paper based upon survey data. Despite its limitations, Glenn still deemed the survey data as evidence against the view — dominant among social scientists — that everything is going well with contemporary marriage. In this view, couples who divorce are not rejecting the institution of marriage, but rather just a particular marriage. On the other hand, some analysts feel that the value structure that undergirds marriage is disintegrating and that as it is deinstitutionalized, marriage will become extremely weakened or perhaps even disappear from contemporary societies. Glenn confessed that he no longer believed that the evidence supported the optimistic view of marriage which he had himself previously held. He was sure that a larger percent of the rising generation would remain single than in the past. He even conceded the possibility of "the beginnings of deinstitutionalization" of marriage.

Looking at the survey evidence, Glenn traced a persistent relationship between marital happiness and personal happiness, especially for women. That is, a good marriage appears to be a necessary but not sufficient condition for personal happiness. But as marital success has grown increasingly hard to achieve, fewer American women have achieved personal happiness. Indeed, Glenn traced much of the recent decline in the psychological well being of American women to a decline in the marriage rate and to decreased satisfaction within marriage. On the other hand, never-married men now report considerably greater happiness than never-married men in the early 1970's. Such survey evidence had gradually caused Glenn to distrust as "overly sanguine" the views of commentators who say that changes in American marriage are simply adaptation to change. Glenn feared that the institution of marriage is in "a great deal of trouble." Going beyond the evidence, Glenn speculated that once people realize the probability of failure in marriage, it will be very difficult for them to commit themselves fully to marriage by making the sacrifices and the investments of time and energy necessary to make a successful marriage. And once couples make only tentative commitments to their marriages, many of those marriages are doomed to fail. Glenn even ventured that perhaps ignorance does have positive social functions in the case of couples who marry unaware of the recent evidence showing how likely it is that their union will fail.

"Wasn't marriage always the triumph of hope over experience?"

Popenoe asked.

In his prepared response to Professor Glenn's paper, Nock focused on the "hedonistic" evaluation of marriage in contemporary America. "Hedonistic marriage is evaluated by the contribution it makes to individual happiness. Marriage is perhaps then simply the sum of its parts, not more." This devaluation of marriage has made possible alarming changes in domestic-relations law, undermining the common-law principle of marital unity. For instance, courts now do permit spouses to testify against one another in serious criminal cases, even in some tort actions. On the other hand, it is growing harder to find states permitting an aggrieved spouse to sue an adulterer under the legal principle of consortium, which defines marriage as a form of symbolic property. Nock listed marital harmony as yet a third endangered principle of domestic-relations law. In the past, the principle of marital harmony meant that disputes in the family were not allowed in the court. In recent years, however, the courts have allowed spouses to sue one another (for rape or abuse, for instance). Some states have even permitted children to sue their parents. The cumulative effect of these legal changes is to exacerbate the individualization of marriage described in Professor Glenn's paper.

Nock interpreted below-replacement-level fertility in the United States — an historical novelty — as further evidence of increasing hedonism in marriage. According to recent estimates, between 25 and 30 percent of baby boomers will remain childless. Nock endorsed the argument that since marriages always go through intervals in which there are no positive attractions, such unions will only endure if some barriers to divorce remain which do not depend upon gratification of pleasure. Children, religious principles, or even financial investments may create such barriers. Nock deplored the fact that there are fewer and fewer nonhedonistic aspects of marriage and fewer and fewer marital rewards not tied directly to personal gratification. While allowing for the possibility that some things (such as education or greater occupational freedom) may compensate for the decline in happiness in marriage, Nock nonetheless found Glenn's conclusion "very ominous" in its implication that marriage is weakening as an institution.

Douglas conjectured that the downward trend in marital success might be not only self-perpetuating, but auto-catalytic as well. He observed that in social relations there exists something like "a tipping point," similar to that defined in chaos theory, a point where basic conceptions change. The concept of a "critical mass" in nuclear physics defines another analogy. Douglas regarded the use of pre-nuptial contracts as evidence that such a tipping point has been reached in contemporary attitudes toward marriage. The distrust implicit in such contracts is tremendously corrosive and breeds further distrust.

Christensen believed that the failure of contemporary marriages could partly be accounted for by unrealistic expectations. Borrowing from literary critic J. Hillis Miller, he noted how in late Victorian fiction the search for the ideal mate replaced the search for God. People can only be disappointed if they enter marriage supposing that it will be bliss and joy and that it will solve every problem. Paradoxically, lower expectations for marriage may mean greater real happiness.

Adding to the catalogue of reasons for marital failure, Popenoe suggested that many young people who want to marry wait so long looking for an ideal mate that they become very accustomed to a single lifestyle, so growing more consumerist and less child-oriented.

Neely worried about the relative importance of marriage for men and women at a time when so many women are in the labor market. He saw fewer marital benefits for women than for men since even among cohabiting professionals women end up doing about 90 percent of the housework. When a woman is in the paid labor market, what is the advantage of living with a man who will say, "By the way, when you get through cleaning the floor, how about sewing this button on?"

Nabers Cabaniss explained contemporary women's choices as responses to two competing impulses. On the one hand, women and men feel a fundamental, relational desire to love and to receive love — a motive Cabaniss suggested might be more fundamentally female than male. On the other hand, men and women seek self-fulfillment outside of relationships, primarily through work and accomplishment. However, these two impulses come into conflict. Cabaniss hoped that both men and women will recognize the futility of looking for self-fulfillment exclusively through work and will realize the need for the fulfillment which can only be found in giving and receiving love.

When Neely asked whether women *want* to work outside the

home, Kasun ventured that women are split 50-50 in their attitudes. Kasun reported that her own two daughters, both holders of
advanced degrees, hold different attitudes about employment and
face different challenges as a consequence. The employed daughter
is physically exhausted by the long hours competing in the workplace
while trying also to perform the housework. However, the other
daughter is being demoralized by the negative social pressure of
people who view her decision to be a housewife as a sign of
incompetence.

Popenoe doubted whether American women are really split 50-
50 in their attitudes toward work. He recalled recent research
finding that 75 percent of women either were in the labor force
recently or intend to enter the labor force when their children are
older. Relatively few women, Popenoe suggested, never want to be
in the work force.

Offering a different statistical answer to the question of whether
women want to work, Christensen cited a recent Princeton survey
which found that among employed mothers with children under
the age of 12, about two-thirds would prefer to work fewer hours in
order to spend more time at home.

Neely called for a social restoration of the woman who chooses
homemaking rather than employment. He noted that it was women
who stay home who raise money for school projects, go with
children on field trips, and do other such community service. Yet
such women receive very little public recognition for their labors
from employed women, who seem unable to understand why they
don't find a job and do something useful.

Glenn objected that no one could encourage women to stay at
home without ignoring the current instability of marriage. At a
time of high divorce rates, it is hazardous for a young woman to stay
out of the labor force.

Nock remarked that sociologists had in recent years asserted
that the movement of women into the labor force had helped push
divorce rates up, while at the same time economists had argued
that women were entering the labor force in anticipation of divorce.

Douglas underscored this point, noting that women must take
work seriously at a time when the average age for marriage is rising
and when approximately two-thirds of new marriages in his home
state of California are headed for divorce.

Smith questioned the realism of young people approaching

marriage. Citing surveys in which college women were asked about their future plans, he saw a range of ambitions — marriage, raising children, work — that would not fit within a 24-hour day. To account for current family patterns, Smith cited Richard Easterlin's theory that a person's material aspirations are largely shaped by childhood experience. Thus, the Americans who were children during the Depression and came of age during World War II had seen scarcity, but found lives of relative abundance. These Americans raised large families on the wages of a single male breadwinner. On the other hand, American men who were born in the 1950's grew up in relative prosperity, but must now really hustle and send their wives to work to enjoy the same relative income.

Although Easterlin claims this generational experience is cyclic, so that the next generation will devote itself more to family life, Smith could not see it that way. Instead, he supposed that once women moved into the labor force, social incentives would shift in a way that would make it hard to ratchet back into earlier patterns. Still, Smith expressed sympathy for the plight of the homemaker, since there are negative social pressures associated with dropping out of the labor force for "too long" after the birth of a child.

Invoking a broader historical perspective, Vinovskis stressed the distinction between the employment of women and the employment of *married* women. During the 19th century, most women worked from the age of 14, 15, or earlier until their early 20's, but stopped working when they married. Although many of these 19th-century women did not care for their circumstances in the labor force, Vinovskis argued that a high percentage of them wanted to work and were not simply driven into the labor force by economic necessity. For such women, marriage was very constricting, because it occasioned societal and cultural pressures to drop out of the labor force.

Turning to the contemporary scene, Vinovskis detected a growing ambivalence about work. A large number of high school students now work, even though their employment typically hurts their studies. On the other hand, a sizable portion of the population does not wish to be employed at all. And at a time when an increasing number of women are entering the labor force, a rising number of men are opting for early retirement.

Neely supposed that the movement of women into paid employment might leave a fundamental task undone within marriage. Is it true, he asked Vitz, that by nature men are not particularly oriented toward family life and that women must domesticate them? If it is true, could it be that fewer women now understand that they must do 90 percent of what it takes to make a marriage work in order to domesticate their mates?

Vitz saw new financial pressures, not untamed male impulses, as the chief problem facing married couples. Women have always worked in the past, he said, citing his own mother and grandmother as examples, but in farm labor they were partners with their husbands. No longer partners, husband and wife must now cope with the financial and logistical challenge of keeping two jobs going. Vitz also complained of a lack of social and cultural support for a father's status. Newspapers now condescendingly refer to married men as "hubby," he observed.

Fleming shared Vitz's doubts that marriages were failing because men were not being domesticated. A cross-cultural survey of the world, he asserted, would provide little evidence that men are naturally macho beasts that women must lasso and tame into marriage.

Attacking a quite different misconception, Fleming faulted as inadequate the modern conception of marriage — traceable to such figures as John Locke and Adam Smith — as a contractual relationship entered into to achieve such objectives as the fostering of mutual happiness and the rearing of children. Fleming urged a reconsideration of an older (and also, curiously, more recent) understanding of the family as an organic entity in which the identities of individuals are to some extent merged. The ancient version of this conception was articulated by Aristotle, who said that a man who achieved every success in his life could still not be regarded as happy if calamity overtook his family after his death. Sociobiology has recently developed a modern version of this notion that a man's welfare is bound up with the welfare of those closest to him. According to sociobiological theory, our interest in our fellows is directly proportioned to our shared genetic heritage. From both Aristotelian and sociobiological perspectives, the family must be regarded as a whole in ways not acknowledged by modern theories which focus on the competing interests of individuals.

Vinovskis did not care to follow biological theory very far in explaining family life. He argued that in the past people often made no distinction between family and household, even though the household included servants and other non-kin. Nor could biology account for the fact that the father — not the mother — was regarded as the natural caregiver in the 15th, 16th, and 17th centuries. Not until the 19th century was the mother strongly identified as the natural caregiver. This fluidity in family institutions makes it hard to identify any past pattern in family life as inherently natural or ideal.

Douglas thought there was more to the idea of a natural role of mothering than Vinovskis allowed. In almost all known societies, he observed, mothers provide most of the loving and care for young children. The father becomes more important only as children become older. The father in most traditional societies assumes responsibility for initiating his sons into the rituals of his people, particularly those that mark a young man as a worthy participant in warfare or the hunt.

Suggesting a revision to Vinovskis' earlier comment on the employment of women during the 19th century, Douglas remarked that in most areas of the country unmarried women who went to work did work at home for factories or they typically performed household labors in homes where they still lived within a family and where their employer still held authority over them *in loco parentis*. American women of the 19th century did not often pursue individual careers outside the confines of family life, except among the upper class, especially in New England, New York, and other industrialized areas.

Reverting to a theme raised by Fleming, Day postulated a split between the kin world and the non-kin world, a split which may make it inappropriate to superimpose economic or even psychological models upon family life. In this split between the kin and non-kin world, Day detected not only a theoretical problem, but a personal tragedy (defined as a problem that does not have a solution) for women who are almost forced to choose between seeking self-fulfillment and entering into that special world of kin.

To document the impossibility of reconciling all the competing interests now motivating young women, Day reported on a survey recently conducted at Washington State University. In this survey, young women in college were asked how they expected to be spending their lives in five years, estimating how many hours they would be devoting in a typical future week to various kinds of activities such as child care, work, shopping, and other pursuits. In a sense, the survey tricked the young women by not giving them a place to tally up the hours they were committing to in their hypothetical future. These young women wanted to have careers, but they also wanted to have families of more than three children, whom they would care for themselves. They intended to do all the heavy and light housekeeping with little help from husbands. They also intended to do five to ten hours of service in the community. They were going to try to do it all, cramming 100-140 hours of activity into a hypothetical future week only 168 hours long. In these fantastic ambitions, Day saw the tragedy of young women who have an impossible double or triple tracking in mind.

Mattox worried that the future conflicts in these young women's lives would be increasingly difficult to resolve. He reasoned that once women have established themselves as full-time employees in the work-place, they put themselves in competition with men, so driving down everyone's wages, making it harder for families to reduce their dependence on wives' earnings. Consequently, women who realize that they are trying to do too much are more likely to reduce their efforts at home, because it has become economically impossible to cut back their commitment to paid employment.

In the same spirit, Day complained of the overwhelming pressure pushing many women — including his own wife, mother of five children — into undesired competition in the non-kin world. He observed tremendous strain on women who live at cross purposes, staying at home when they would prefer to work or working when they would prefer to stay at home.

But Neely quibbled with Mattox over whether it was the movement of women into the labor force which has driven down wages in the United States. In Neely's analysis, wages had fallen because a new international competition has replaced the oligopolistic market formerly enjoyed by car manufacturers and other American industries. Neely observed that while wages have been declining among the American lower class, they have actually been climbing among those who process abstract ideas. He judged that among those who process such ideas, it was still possible for a family to live perfectly well on one income, so long as they lived in someplace like Rockford, Illinois, or Charleston, West Virginia, rather than downtown New York City.

Douglas objected that wages had not declined simply because America's oligopolies disappeared. Rather, the unprecedented growth of the bureaucratic state has eroded the efficiency of the economy in general, while increasing the tax burden for the nation's families.

Responding to a query from Fleming, Nock surveyed recent changes in the legal status of the family. Educated in Louisiana, Nock's early perspective was shaped by the peculiarity of that state's legal heritage as a Napoleonic Code state, not a common law state. In the Napoleonic Code, there are no individuals in a marriage; marriage is a unity. Even in common law, marriage exists for many purposes as a unity beyond the individuals who are married. However, Nock discerned a growing tendency in the United States to define marriage in law as two individuals with individual interests which often may conflict. He cited interspousal suits as the most obvious illustration of this new legal conception of marriage, but he also noted the bizarre cases of children suing parents for malpractice. Judging it a disastrous trend, Nock lamented that the sense of marital unity was losing legal ground to this new understanding of marriage as two individuals. Although he could not tell whether no-fault divorce laws should be counted as a cause or a consequence of this new conception of the family, Nock was sure the two were closely linked.

On the theme of intrafamilial lawsuits, Fleming complained about an International Declaration of Children's Rights now being debated in the United Nations. He found it troubling that the Reagan Administration had sought in the framing of this declaration to give children the choice to emigrate with or without their parents — as in the famous Walter Polovchak case. The international enactment of such a doctrine would say that children could in effect divorce their parents and move abroad.

As a justice informed about such issues, Neely intervened to clarify what actually happens in cases in which parental or spousal immunity is abrogated. In most such cases, he reported, the decisive consideration is the need to collect from an insurance company that will not pay medical or other expenses unless a largely fictive suit is filed by one spouse against the other or by children against parents. Except in wild, crazy places like the Far West, Neely reported no real suits between spouses who plan to continue their marriage. On the other hand, divorce cases often lead to lengthy property suits.

Shifting the legal focus, Neely speculated that if the Supreme

Court retreated from the *Roe* v. *Wade* decision [this conference was held before the *Webster* decision was handed down], it would have very far-reaching political implications because the left wing of the women's movement could no longer keep their highest priority out of political bargaining. He noted that in her recent examination of the question, Mary Ann Glendon of Harvard had found relatively little controversy surrounding abortion in Europe, because as abortion policies were developed there, almost everyone's sense of outrage had been accommodated within the political process. In this country, however, left-wing feminists have been free to focus on strange and perverse issues because their bread-and-butter issues — abortion under *Roe* v. *Wade* and employment rights under Title VII — have been largely taken off the political table. He anticipated that if the Supreme Court retreated from *Roe* v. *Wade*, feminists would have to make political trades and compromises in new ways. Such political compromises would likely effect dramatic changes in many legal policies that affect women. Neely characterized feminists as a group that worries not about what women really do, but about what an elite group of women fantasize that women might do. Rather than continue to thumb their noses at traditionalists, feminists would have to try to be more supportive of their choices.

Mattox predicted that a repeal of *Roe* v. *Wade* would affect conservatives as well as feminists, as voters on the right discover they must make some sacrifices in order to achieve a politically feasible consensus. The result would be greater moderation and less polarization.

Stepping back from these short-term political considerations, Douglas discerned a tidal drift in Western thinking about the family. Since ancient times, the family has been conceived of as a separate level of reality — like *res publica* — which was separate and beyond the existence of individuals. In its own way, the myth of Romantic Love — the myth of a preordained union of souls — reinforced the belief in the inviolate sanctity of the family. Douglas viewed *Roe* v. *Wade*, in which the Court tried to define by law the very meaning of existence, of personhood, as a particularly astounding illustration of a modern mode of thought subversive of the sanctity of family life. Modern thinking rests not upon the ancient premise that family life is sacred, but upon a rational and hedonistic calculation of individual advantage. Changes in the law affected this kind of thinking at the margin, but the cultural drift was beyond the governance of lawyers and judges.

Christensen identified day care as an institution which fits into the general retreat from marriage. Citing an article by Nock, he argued that among nontraditional women, motherhood increasingly resembles fatherhood in that both mean simply the provision of financial resources for a child. "Why," Christensen asked, "would two fathers be married to one another?" Day care, he remarked, erodes the complementarity of the sexes by creating a class of professionals to care for children, while women enter the paid work force with men.

Christensen questioned the term "quality day care," suspecting that what it actually means is paying and training workers enough so that they love the children they care for. When in another context money changes hands and we call it love, he said, I think we know what it really is. Remembering an argument from philosopher Alasdair MacIntyre, Christensen identified a tension between the pursuit of moral excellence and the pursuit of social efficiency. He conceded the social inefficiency of maternal child care, especially for a mother who is highly trained; yet, he felt such inefficiency was the necessary price of the fostering of loving bonds which are at the heart of the family. Recalling a consultation on day care sponsored by The Rockford Institute in December 1988 (see *Day Care: Child Psychology and Adult Economics*), Christensen reported research by Jay Belsky finding that full-time non-maternal care for infants poses a risk of weakened emotional bonding. Although there is more controversy about older children, some studies have uncovered evidence of heightened aggression among preschoolers in day care. In a study recently completed at the University of Texas, researchers found that on every measure used — grades, teacher evaluations, relationships with peers, parents' reports — third graders who had been in day care as preschoolers were worse off than third graders who had not. Still, Christensen despaired of resolving debates over day care through the accumulation of empirical studies. Belsky had complained that many of his professional colleagues criticized him for publishing studies which might make people feel guilty. Further, some psychologists interpret weakened bonding between mother and child, often caused by day care, as the development of a precocious and desirable autonomy.

When Schoen wondered about the economics of day care and the need for subsidy, Smith cited research concluding that employed mothers pay on average about 25 percent of their salary for day care, no matter what their salary. Venturing a broader comment on the economics of day care, Neely argued that the need to subsidize day care depends upon the type of work in which the mother is employed. If a mother can operate a word processor or has received some other type of training that is in high demand, then she can probably pay for day care without government subsidy. Especially in the labor-starved Northeast, many companies are now beginning to establish on-site day-care centers as a way to attract employees. Neely did not regard the costs of these centers as a subsidy, since the economics of labor supply would dictate those costs would not exceed the costs of attracting other workers if the company did not establish a day-care center. On the other hand, in the case of "Jesse Jackson's woman" — the woman who works every day in unskilled labor — if government does not subsidize day care, she may not be able to find care for her child and may be compelled to stay home on welfare — an option already attractive to many.

Vinovskis thought it impossible to assess day care without considering the responsibility of the state to alleviate poverty. He lamented that the retreat from marriage has plunged many children — the offspring of unmarried or divorced parents — into poverty.

From a strictly economic viewpoint, Kasun could see no justification for day care that is provided or subsidized by the government, since day care is not a public good nor is it collectively consumed. The only person for whom day care can be economically efficient is the woman who earns more than her babysitter. As a matter of personal judgment rather than economic analysis, Kasun thought that a poor mother should be given financial support to stay home to care for her own children. Kasun expressed personal annoyance over proposed policies which would subsidize day care for affluent two-income families, while imposing heavier tax burdens on traditional households in which the mother stays home to care for her own children. Such policies struck her as patently unfair. Fairness required that people be fully informed about day care — including the risks for children — then exercise and pay for their own free choice. Kasun felt that young mothers need to understand that full-time motherhood is one of the most difficult and challenging yet rewarding pursuits in life.

Neely objected to the inadequacy of Kasun's economic analysis. Consider, he proposed, the case of a secretary he knows who makes $21,000 a year, who spends $3,000 a year on child care, and finds it tough to get by financially. She wants the state to take over the costs of her child care — costs far less than supporting her on welfare — so that she can survive at her current job. Such thinking, shared by a large political lobby, is essentially redistributionist, Neely argued, but is not as irrational as Kasun's analysis suggested.

Kasun countered that what was needed was not a subsidy of day care, but rather a nondiscriminatory tax credit for all families to be used for child care or for whatever else the family needs.

Day care defined a secondary question for Vinovskis, who urged consideration of the broader question of how to help the poor, especially children growing up in single-parent households. He especially faulted policymakers who fail to recognize the financial responsibilities of fathers, who should be legally compelled to pay child support for the first eighteen years of their children's lives, whether or not they are married to the mothers.

Neely protested that his experience as a judge has taught him that it is often difficult to find fathers. Even when an irresponsible father is found, he often jumps from job to job in a way that makes it impossible to attach his wages. Besides, in many cases an unmarried father may not care if failure to pay child support lands him in jail — at an annual cost of $27,000 to the taxpayer.

Vinovskis responded that aside from these extreme cases, a system for collecting child support would work with a great many middle-class men. Something has to be done, he pleaded, to end the national disgrace of fathers failing to pay child support.

Day saw little hope for Vinovskis' plan, pointing out that a high percentage of divorcing husbands are young men whose earnings are so low that judges could not press very much out of them. Besides, under the provisions of no-fault divorce, the judge cannot lean very hard on a husband if his wife has the same capacity to earn an income.

Not willing to give up, Vinovskis reasoned that even if a man earns very little during the first years of a child's life, he will likely earn more as the child grows.

Not persuaded, Neely objected that it still costs more to collect child support than it's worth. The impracticality of collecting child support persists despite the enactment a few years ago of an amendment to the Social Security Act requiring all states to improve their systems for collecting child support. In Neely's view, women who are not receiving child support need a state officer who would prepare their petitions for them, so that irresponsible fathers would be brought into court as soon as they fall behind in their child-support payments. However, that is not how the National Organization for Women (NOW) has approached the issue. NOW advocated the creation of a system of "law masters" or "domestic relations judges" to hear divorce and child-support cases. As matters have worked out, these judges spend all of their time hearing divorce disputes, leaving no manpower to prepare the petitions to collect child support.

Vinovskis countered that studies at the Institute on Poverty at the University of Wisconsin and elsewhere demonstrate the economic feasibility of collecting child support. In Sweden, he reported, government officials have developed an effective system for identifying fathers and holding them financially responsible for their children.

Douglas feared any further intervention of the state bureaucracy into the family. As with any criminal, we need to understand the motives and morality of a father who evades financial responsibility for his children. These motives can be partially clarified by considering a father's rights and authority in the family now contrasted with those rights and authority in the past. In large part because of the intrusion of the state into home life, a man may exert very little moral authority even if he discovers his wife in an extramarital affair. A violent response to such betrayal will land him in court for spouse abuse. Likewise, the father who tries to stop a child's use of drugs by beating will be cited for child abuse. Especially among the poor, fathers find themselves at the mercy of state officials, denied any moral authority in their own right. The consequence is a growing number of fathers who feel that their children are not theirs.

For illustration, Fleming recounted the case of the Hispanic father in Chicago whose son had lain brain dead in coma, kept alive by life-support systems for six months after swallowing a balloon at a birthday party. To no avail, he had pleaded with state officials to let his baby die so that he could go home to God. Finally, the father pulled a gun on the nurse, made her leave the room, and cradled the baby in his arms until he died. Although the coroner did not return a finding of homicide, the state's attorney threatened to prosecute the father for murder.

Returning to the question of collecting child support, Vitz joined the chorus of pessimists. He predicted that if something like Vinovskis' plan for collecting child support were enforced, it would exacerbate the retreat from marriage.

When Vinovskis pressed him for his own policy prescriptions, Douglas admitted he had few practical suggestions, since he believed society was headed for major catastrophies that would force some of these issues to be sorted out in their wake. But if he were to propose policy, Douglas would recommend a general reduction in state bureaucracy.

The father of a child is definitely responsible for the child, but the local community — not the government — should enforce that responsibility through informal means. Douglas traced many social pathologies to state officials who repeatedly tell poor people they are not responsible for their problems, that society caused their problems.

Although sharing Douglas' preference for informal rather than government solutions, Fleming thought that at least in the short run the responsibility for collecting child support must fall to government. Such collection could be accomplished by local and county officials, however, rather than through a state or federal network. But no political, legal, or ethical system may be based upon duties without rights, any more than such a system may be based upon rights without duties. He observed that over the past century, the traditional rights of fathers have declined. For instance, the state now mandates how a father must educate his children, while limiting his authority to impose corporal punishment upon his children. To take an extreme case, Fleming cited an argument advanced by George Swan at a previous Rockford Institute conference on "The Family Wage" (see *The Family Wage: Work, Gender, and Children in the Modern Economy*). Swan pointed out that under current abortion law, a father has no right even to determine whether his child is born. Imagine the case of the man who proposes marriage to his pregnant girlfriend, but she refuses, saying she is having an abortion instead. Then she does not have the abortion, nor does she marry; yet, she still expects the unmarried father to support her child. Without some rehabilitation of the authority of fathers, Fleming resisted any plan for enforcing greater financial responsibility.

Speaking in defense of government bureaucracy, Neely cited horrible instances of abuse in which state officials must intervene to protect children. In one recent case in West Virginia, a child was beaten to death with a paddle by religious fanatics. While state officials in West Virginia hold a fairly high presumption in favor of parents, Neely thought it essential that the state wield some authority to intervene in cases of vicious and brutal abuse.

Douglas thought it important to remember that in a disproportionate number of cases, those guilty of child abuse — especially sexual abuse — are stepparents or cohabiting boyfriends. The media, he complained, has failed to report this pattern, so helping to turn child abuse into a legal weapon against fatherhood. Douglas outlined a vicious cycle, as state intervention solves some local problems for a time but thereby creates bigger problems over time, so requiring an expansion of the state system, ad infinitum. Eventually, he predicted, the whole thing will collapse, forcing people to reconstitute society based on informal order.

Popenoe demurred, pointing out that during the last century Americans have lost the small community which originally surrounded the family. A century ago, if parents had abused their children, relatives and neighbors would immediately have gone into the house to stop it. Community pressure then governed parental conduct. Popenoe judged it essential that the state develop replacements for the community pressure which no longer exists.

Fleming rejected this line of reasoning, asserting that the centralization of state power was deliberate, not accidental. States had, for instance, first centralized their educational apparatus, then purposefully set out to destroy community schools.

Nonsense, Popenoe rejoined. This country has the most decentralized, localized educational system in the industrial world. If there is any single reason our education system fails, it is that it is so decentralized. Popenoe thought it unrealistic to believe that education could now be reformed by handing all power back to local school districts, as if they were some kind of natural human community.

Douglas gloomily predicted that American schools would grow ever-more centralized, causing even more inefficiency and ideological thinking. Against Popenoe's assertions, Douglas voiced a basic faith in the goodness and rationality of human beings, who would reorganize their lives sensibly if state powers were abolished.

Confessing considerable sympathy with anarchists, Christensen nonetheless feared that Douglas was indulging in naiveté. I believe the state is evil, he said, but a necessary evil. The problem comes when politics become utopian, so defining the state as a mechanism for building heaven on earth.

From his position in government, Neely could not see much utopianism or romanticism among state officials, most of whom simply try to muddle through.

But after the revolution is over, Fleming interrupted, passionate ideological commitments are no longer necessary. State functionaries can then simply muddle through.

Unperturbed, Neely explained that Franklin Roosevelt really had made the world a better place. Those who grew up in his shadow supposed they could go on making the world a better place. Instead, what they discovered were insoluble problems, problems like the Charles Murray phenomenon of unintended effects, of perverse effects. Neely compared the problem of unintended effects to the Heisenberg principle in physics: setting out to measure the speed of the electron, the scientist unintentionally changes that speed by measuring it. People in government today — unlike people in academia and perhaps even people in the media — are quite unideological and nonpartisan. Things were not always so. Neely recalled a period of romanticism in government in the 1960's and the beginning of the 1970's when people really believed they could change things. But America is today in a period of retrenchment, aptly symbolized by the nonideological Bush Administration. George Bush, Neely joked, makes General McClellan in the War Between the States look impetuous.

Rejoining the dispute over the state, Popenoe remarked that when in Europe, he tends to argue against the state; when in the U.S., he tends to argue in favor of the state. It is a matter of degree. How is it, he asked, that this country suffers from rates of child abuse and spouse abuse that run about ten times higher than in other developed countries, yet our state is about ten times weaker than that of these other societies?

Fleming accounted for the relatively high level of violence in America by noting the incredible ethnic diversity in the United

States. In a northern European state such as Sweden, the people are much more homogenous, bound together by ethnic continuity, by a common religion, and by shared values. In contrast, the United States sometimes resembles a set of warring tribes. In Dade County, Florida, for instance, ethnic warfare often erupts between blacks and Hispanics. Such problems don't exist in Minnesota.

Although Popenoe conceded that ethnic diversity might account for some of the violence in America, he urged Fleming to reconsider the role of the state.

Douglas could not accept Popenoe's position that the American state was much more underdeveloped than European states. After all, American government at all levels controls about 40 percent of the economy compared to 50-55 percent in most of the European countries, 60 percent in Sweden.

Opening the third session of the conference, Douglas admitted that he had adopted an unusual, even off-color tone in his paper to force participants to realize that normal procedures produce normal results, results that are unsatisfactory. It was time for Americans to start looking for ways to escape from the iron cage of modern rationalistic bureaucracy. Douglas conceded that this was difficult, especially for professionals who have spent their lives learning how to live inside the cage. Perhaps it was hubris on his part to suppose that by adopting an off-color tone in his paper he could inspire others to see the constraints of the cage in a way that they normally do not. Douglas was annoyed that in most of the major sociology textbooks, the rising divorce rate and other family miseries are depicted as merely short-run symptoms of the transition to greater social happiness. Citing William O'Neill's book *Divorce in the Progressive Era*, Douglas noted that people were arguing that divorce would make everyone happier even when the annual divorce rate stood at only seven-tenths of one divorce per thousand Americans. Since then, divorce rates have climbed almost 700 percent. The vexing question remains: What is causing all this? During the first one hundred years of their profession, sociologists always blamed urbanization. Then the indictment shifted to industrialization. Neither explanation will bear close scrutiny. Urbanization plateaued some time ago, has even receded. Likewise, industrialization plateaued long ago: roughly 20 percent of our economy remains in industry. Accordingly, experts went on to other specific explanations of the breakdown of the family, each pursuing his own professional specialty. Douglas' own view was that the tide of family disintegration was merely one part of a general drift into social miseries, stagnation, inflation, declining efficiency, litigious-ness, and civil strife. Meanwhile, the Leviathan state grows, as state officials proffer good intentions as justification for the expansion of their power.

Since the time of Sumer and Egypt, Douglas observed, bureau-cratic states have slowly evolved into ever larger, more concentrated structures, eventually provoking a sense of outrage against their tyranny. Such bureaucratic states almost always fall; they do not slowly decay or progressively ratchet down. Such states collapse, ending "with a big bang, not a whimper. The whimperings come after the big bang." Utopianism counts as one of the most potent forces fueling the growth of the Leviathan state, which employs an army of scientific experts to plan the lives of the people, to teach them how to be happy and how to conduct their family lives. Douglas found this utopian reliance upon experts laughable, since the experts and their children live lives in far greater disarray and suffer from worse problems than the people they are trying to help. This pretense goes beyond ancient hubris and leads to blindness and stupidity. Over time, bureaucracies create false incentives for the creation of misinformation, disinformation, so creating even greater inefficiencies in the state.

Of his dire prediction of a general collapse of American society, Douglas joked that in ten years either he would be glad to see that he was wrong or everyone else will have forgotten that he was right. Few social scientists are now looking at the big picture, though. Universities and foundations encourage professors to burrow into ever-smaller specialties. In such a world, it becomes dangerous to take up general themes.

In her prepared response, Kasun praised Douglas' paper as impressive and very moving. Agreeing with Douglas' main points, Kasun offered an economist's perspective on the problems Douglas surveyed. Because they lay great stress on the inviolability and the inscrutability of the individual and because they recognize that the individual is usually acting on behalf of family, economists can offer some hope in this age of disintegration. Gary Becker in particular has helped the world rediscover altruism as that situation in which the individual derives benefit from the belief that he is benefiting others. Assuming that each individual can make rational choices among available options, economists resist the notion that government planners or service professionals can make better choices for individuals. Opposed to bureaucracy, economists find grandiose notions of progress unintelligible. As practitioners of the science of choice, economists do not believe in any inevitable progress toward some inevitable destination. Because they accept the necessity of judging even the most idealistic regimes against economic reality, Kasun argued that economists find it easy to believe that people must face social and moral judgment as well. Kasun also endorsed Douglas' emphasis on ultimate truths, costs, and values. She despaired of the possibility of economic reasoning without a belief in goodness and an eternal standard.

Identifying a possible disagreement with Douglas, Kasun disputed the inevitability of a future catastrophe. Still free to choose, people can turn society around. Economists do not define human beings simply as monetary calculating machines with dollar signs in their eyes, yet they insist that people do respond to financial incentives. The current retreat from family life results not from an inevitable slide into a vicious value system, but instead results from a perverse rearrangement of incentives. People still want to live up to the standards of truth and goodness which undergird family life, but they find it increasingly difficult economically. For instance, parents now bear most of the huge economic cost of raising children, but receive virtually none of the economic benefit of having reared them. Further, Richard Vedder has demonstrated a high statistical correlation between divorce and inflation. Unanticipated inflation sparks family conflict by impoverishing families. Although not as discouraged as Douglas, Kasun conceded powerful forces have rearranged economic incentives. This rearrangement amounts to a war on the traditional family, a war on motherhood, fatherhood, and childhood. She lamented that many of her students had been indoctrinated since grade school in the notion that everything is relative.

Douglas agreed that economic analysis can help explain why bureaucracy grows. Yet Douglas took scant comfort in the freedom of individuals to choose, since the bureaucratic state becomes so all encompassing that it can educate people to think in its terms. Inevitably, bureaucracies distort information, so twisting thought. The judicial fiat removing unborn babies from the definition of life illustrates the power of the state to change basic categories. A strong critic of official information, Douglas constantly seeks to find where it is invalid and unreliable. While physicists often estimate the margin of their errors in the millionths, social scientists routinely operate on data which is unreliable by anywhere from 10 percent to 1000 percent. People may be free within the modern bureaucratic state, but that freedom is powerfully constrained by the information given them. Seeing problems, people do want to respond. Rationally, these people act at the margin of these problems in behavior that works in most everyday life, except when things have gone profoundly wrong. But people shrink from drastic actions, like revolutions. In any case, the bureaucratic state reduces the likelihood of rebellion through disinformation that hides the ultimate costs of its governance. Douglas named the decay of the family as the most profound cost hidden by government disinformation.

Skeptical, Popenoe asked why modernism has advanced furthest in the one developed nation with the weakest bureaucratic structure.

Douglas doubted whether the United States should be characterized as the most modern nation. He conceded that sexual modernism does prevail among educated Americans, although no more than among educated people in other developed countries. Educated Americans and educated Soviets largely agree in sexual modernism. The mass of the Russian people — 40 percent of whom remain peasants — of course do not share the lives of sexual modernists, yet the abortion rate runs high in Moscow, much higher even than in Beverly Hills or New York. In overall outlook, however, Americans espouse less utopian, less modern attitudes than the educated class in the Soviet Union and other communist countries (at least until recently). Guided by common sense, Americans remain less modernist in outlook even than Swedes, although the homogeneity of Sweden makes it unfit to compare to a nation so diverse and pluralistic as the United States. Precisely because they are so divided and combative, Americans fight the state bureaucracy, retarding its growth.

Neely was struck by the tone of near desperation he detected in Douglas' description of ideological thinking at elite universities. Neely acknowledged the existence of such a locked mindset, recalling how he had been picketed ten years ago for acting out a vignette in which the average Japanese man comes home, looks at his wife

and says, "Oh! I was screwed again!" Neely thought it remarkable
that such a small act could generate such outrage. At the University of Charleston where he teaches, Neely found a healthy diversity among the faculty, which includes Catholic priests and right-
wing yellers and screamers like him. If it is true — as Douglas
asserts in his paper — that all the propaganda (in the best sense of
the word) is aimed in one direction at America's top universities,
then we face a serious problem. How, in any case, did all these like-
thinking people, who no longer enjoy the collegiality of yelling and
screaming at each other, ever become concentrated at the top
American universities?

To illustrate the problem, Fleming recounted the case of a friend
of his who failed to win tenure at Miami University of Ohio, a
conservative middle-class school. A revisionist Marxist, his friend
was denounced as a Trotskyite by an orthodox Marxist in the
department who had the votes to keep him out. The chairman of the
department, a Thomist, refused to intervene.

Neely still remained puzzled as to why the university has been
politicized while the rest of the world has grown less political.

Douglas explained that the most intellectually ambitious people,
the people who most yearn for power and fame, gravitate to the
university. Even General Motors does not hire intellectuals to do
sociology of a neo-Marxist or any other sort. Meanwhile, conservative older professors are retiring. Even before retirement, many
have shut down their minds and stopped publishing after winning
tenure. New financial incentives also hasten the radicalization of
the faculty, as Marxists and other radicals capture journals and
professional institutions.

Vitz blamed ideological thinking upon growing bureaucracy
within the university itself. He recalled that 30 or 40 years ago, few
ties bound the universities to the Federal government. Now the
university and the Federal government work hand in glove. Vitz
sees professors shuttling back and forth between the universities,
administrative jobs in government, and research positions at the
National Institute of Mental Health and other positions. In the
process, research scientists come to resemble bureaucrats, chiefly
responsible for administering grants and supervising research
assistants. Vitz thought it symptomatic that most large universities employ at least five or six people devoted entirely to evaluating
research for compliance to bureaucratic standards for treatment of

human or animal subjects. But for Vitz the worst academic consequence of a growing bureaucracy was the stifling of the search for
truth. For instance, Vitz sees clinical psychology masquerading as
a science and being massively funded as a science by the university
bureaucracy. Yet overwhelming evidence now shows that clinical
psychology is not a science. Thirty years ago Vitz could discuss such
questions with his colleagues. Now he cannot even raise the issue
without threatening the vested interests of an entrenched bureaucracy.

Vinovskis protested that Douglas had painted a one-sided picture that distorts the elements of truth it does contain. Although
conceding a liberal bias among most academics, Vinovskis saw
nothing like a monolithic leftist conspiracy. Vinovskis complained
that the apocalyptic vision of Douglas' paper invites only two
responses: either "Amen!" or "You must be kidding!" which he
thought more appropriate. He faulted the paper for indulging in
overblown generalities and for failing to stimulate more critical
analysis or further dialogue about the issues defining the retreat
from marriage. For instance, Vinovskis identified the rise in individualism as a primary cause of the retreat from marriage. But that
rise in individualism began in the late 18th or early 19th centuries,
long before the rise of the bureaucratic state demonized by Douglas.
On the other hand, it is possible to see a growing national state,
increasingly reliant upon the family, in 15th-, 16th-, and 17th-
century England. The relationship between the state and the
family is more complex than Douglas depicts it, Vinovskis asserted.
These complexities may be further uncovered by reexamining the
abortion issue. If a society in which 20-30 percent of conceptions
end in abortion is headed for the Gulag, then what about early 19th-
century America when approximately that situation did prevail
because Americans at that time did not regard abortion before
quickening as a moral issue? During the 19th-century, the medical
profession shifted in attitude and persuaded legislatures and
judges to enact anti-abortion statutes. The state — attacked by
Douglas for fostering abortion — was moving in the opposite
direction in the 19th century.

Christensen shared some of Vinovskis' concern, sensing a kind
of Manichaean passion in Douglas' paper. Modernism, like an
ancient religion, is many things. Modernism does include a destructive bureaucratic impulse, which can be best understood if the

rise of individualism (mentioned by Vinovskis) is viewed within a Hobbesian dialectic. Christensen disputed Hobbes' depiction of "the state of nature" as a state of mercilessly warring egos, arguing instead that "the state of nature" is family life. However, he argued that a decaying culture can produce something resembling Hobbes' state of nature, thus requiring the creation of a strong centralized state of the sort that Hobbes called for as the only means to preserve order.

Fleming questioned Douglas on a technical point, citing the philosophical debate about the existence of altruism (mentioned in Douglas' paper) in the natural world. From a biological perspective, the mother monkey who sacrifices herself for four children is not performing an altruistic act, but rather is benefitting herself genetically. Similarly, it may be argued that there is a difference between sacrifices made for friends and sacrifices made for children, siblings, or cousins. Fleming observed that he could devote all his income to his own personal interests and stop paying for his children's food, clothing, and education. But since his children represent his natural immortality on this planet, such a strategy would be suicidal, while his current scrimping and saving for his children is probably not altruism. On the other hand, when Sir Philip Sidney offered his last drink of water to a dying foot soldier, that constituted altruism.

Returning to an earlier theme, Douglas again emphasized the power of bureaucrats to distort information by shaping definitions. He noted that once blindness became subject to government definition and became a reason for government assistance, bureaucratic agencies sprang up to help newspaper-reading "blind" people.

Intervening as chairman, Carlson asked participants to consider Douglas' central theme: Does the bureaucratic state figure as a unique and peculiarly potent cause of the retreat from marriage — or do the activities of the contemporary state merely reflect a drift in the broader culture?

To gauge the effects of the state upon family life, Fleming offered friendly criticism of Douglas' historical analogies. Although he found Douglas inaccurate and misleading in his discussion of Nazi Germany and Rome at the time of Tacitus, Fleming argued that correcting the errors actually strengthens Douglas' argument that the modern bureaucratic state is weakening the family. At no time, he observed, did the Roman government ever exert anything like the influence which the American government today exerts in family life. Except in the lives of the senatorial aristocracy at Rome, the Roman state had almost no control over the family or its traditions. The power of the Roman state depended heavily on volunteerism within the local governments throughout Italy, Gaul, the Germanic provinces, all the way to Britain, North Africa, and Syria. Even when volunteerism eroded and the Roman government resorted to coercing wealthy local landholders to collect taxes and perform other functions, these officials operated under very broad guidelines and enjoyed remarkable autonomy. Agreeing with Douglas about the growth of bureaucracy, Fleming found the very word *bureaucracy* too tame, since none of the past empires usually called bureaucratic ever practiced the kind of massive intervention into private and communal life now seen in the United States.

Turning to a different historical analogy, Fleming rejected as inapt the comparison of the Holocaust to the current practice of abortion in the United States. Contrasting the two situations reflects both better and worse on us than on the Nazis. The Nazis labeled a certain class of people as subhuman, so giving the state the right to put them in slave-labor camps, which turned into extermination camps. In *Roe* v. *Wade*, the American government redefined the protections afforded unborn children, so allowing people to exercise something like what in Roman times was called *patria potestas*, whereby a father could put a child to death. Douglas' Holocaust analogy would only be justified if the U.S. government actually required women to abort their babies (as the Chinese government now sometimes does). Fleming found the rising rates of abortion in the United States terrifying because the government is not forcing Americans to participate in this destruction of life. No storm troopers are kicking in the doors of pregnant women, yet many Americans have morally, socially, and culturally embraced the practice.

Challenging Douglas and Fleming, Nock posited a strong correlation between individual freedom and privacy, arguing that while the state may have grown in the world, that growth has not necessarily harmed privacy and freedom. For comparison he recalled how during the colonial era, tithing men made a weekly survey of all families as an obligation of citizenship. Each family was then required to announce any visitor in the home. All strangers in the community were registered. Residential construction of the time did not allow for much privacy, nor did the presence in typical households of boarders and lodgers, servants and maids. Nock rejoiced in the greater privacy enjoyed by Americans. In traditional communities, privacy was limited not by the state, but by neighbors. Without such a community, privacy is limited by the state. But since the state ultimately proves less effective in curtailing privacy, it therefore in a sense guarantees greater personal freedom. Consequently, Nock strongly disagreed that the growth of the state has meant less personal freedom.

Elaborating on Nock's theme, Smith ventured that personal privacy has expanded in modern life as the controls of family life have weakened. If privacy is a virtue, then the disintegration of family life has helped to guarantee that virtue.

Carlson wondered if Smith was not confusing *privacy* with *individualism*.

Fleming stressed the distinction between informal social controls that operate within traditional societies and the legal controls imposed by the state. He compared informal community controls to the restraints imposed in dealing with in-laws: such controls may prove irritating and chafing, but they are still quite different from directives from an armed police state.

Christensen assessed the modern rise of privacy less favorably than Nock. He recalled how in *The Great Divorce*, C.S. Lewis depicted hell as a huge gray city in which people live about a block apart, because they cannot stand one another. Christensen supposed that this dubious privacy develops naturally with the growth of the bureaucratic state, as may be seen in contemporary Sweden, a country with a huge bureaucratic state and (according to recent figures) the smallest average household size in the world.

Returning to the abortion debate, Neely criticized as cavalier those who oppose abortion without taking into account the problems of bringing into the world children who are going to suffer nothing but misery. He asserted that most of the children who are aborted are children who would have no chance to any kind of quality life. What opportunities lie open, he asked, to the child of an unmarried 17-year-old girl living in the inner city? He dismissed the existing social safety net as inadequate in such circumstances, since the people now dependent upon it are already creating an underclass that is growing progressively worse. The severity of the problem may be seen by the unprecedented failure — the refusal —

of the underclass to take jobs at a time when jobs are opening up in phenomenal numbers, especially in the Northeast. Given this enormous cultural deficit evident in the underclass, how can Americans talk about swelling its ranks by perhaps a million a year by outlawing abortion? Placing himself in John Rawls's hypothetical "original position" of ignorance as to where he might be born into society, Neely saw no reason why he would want to be born into such a world. Surveying the global perspective, Neely challenged Kasun's view that population growth does not constitute a problem. He recalled teaching law in Shanghai, a city so crowded that at any time during the day the entire downtown looks like the West Virginia University football stadium immediately after the Penn State game. Perhaps Vermont or West Virginia could absorb another half a million people, but in most of the world, people are a big, big problem.

Fleming poured sarcasm on Neely's analysis of abortion, hailing extermination of the underclass as a brilliant solution to their economic plight. But why stop with the unborn underclass? Why not wipe out the underclass up to, say, age twelve?

In more measured response to Neely's abortion arguments, Kasun confessed that as an economist she could read no one else's mind and therefore could not impose any definition for "quality of life" on others. A person who does not like the quality of his life has the power to end it for himself without someone else doing that for him, Kasun reasoned. Kasun likewise rejected the crowdedness of Shanghai as a justification for Draconian population controls, arguing that some of the most crowded areas in the world are also some of the most prosperous. Taiwan, for instance, is several times more crowded than the mainland and possesses fewer natural resources yet still produces five times the gross national product per capita.

Global implications aside, Carlson saw the desire among American couples to diminish their fertility as a development linked to the retreat from marriage. He judged it historically new and unusual that many couples now regard the bearing of a child as a negative act.

Neely acknowledged that until a few years ago he had regarded restraining the size of one's family as a moral obligation, even for those with the economic resources to support a large family. Father of two children, Neely admitted that if he were younger he would want a third child, in part because of evidence that the nation's intellectual class is not replacing itself.

But before leaving the abortion debate, Neely appealed to those present to realize that conservatives will need to make political concessions on the issue in order to prevail on other critical questions — such as the value of long-term stability of marriage, the indispensability of a two-parent family for children's mental health, the avoidability of all but 15-20 percent of divorces, and the relative undesirability of most wives' working outside the home. The successful articulation of such issues will be jeopardized if conservatives persist in comparing abortion to the Holocaust or talk about population control as merely one more intrusion into the autonomy of the family. Such arguments become like the 13th chime of a ridiculous clock, a chime which is not only in and of itself absurd, but which creates doubt about the validity of the other twelve chimes.

Fleming responded that *Roe* v. *Wade* was reprehensible because murder laws should not be regulated by the Federal government. Fleming expressed willingness to participate in the kind of politically brokered compromises urged by Neely, but brokering could not begin until the states regained authority over the issue.

Reverting to an earlier theme, Carlson asked whether in truth the state was undermining the family or whether, instead, the state is compensating for family failures. Is the family now no longer willing to carry its burden or to assume responsibility for its freedom?

Popenoe felt that enough energy had been expended bashing state bureaucracy. Wasn't it time to bash capitalism for its part in undermining the family? For a number of reasons, the family is in decline, making many of the activities of the state essential as a way of picking up the pieces. Among industrialized societies, family decline appears most accentuated in the United States, which has the weakest state bureaucracy in the industrialized world, and in the European welfare states, which have the strongest state bureaucracies. The breakup of families in European welfare states does not create as many painful consequences as in the United States, because of state services. Why are American families falling apart as fast as those in European welfare states? Popenoe blamed capitalism for creating incentives for family dissolution. Every time a family breaks up, two households form, requiring the purchase of new real estate, new home appliances, and other goods. Driven by the profit motive, capitalists find advantage in these consequences of family dissolution. Unregulated capitalism further betrays the family in the anti-family themes which permeate popular entertainment. Acknowledging a point of agreement with Douglas, Popenoe conceded that both the growth of the state and the growth of capitalism are associated with the rise of modernism. Yet he faulted Douglas for writing a utopian paper which gives readers not a clue about what to do about the situation — except to wipe out the state. Popenoe expressed confidence that cutting back on the state in America would not yield the results Douglas desired

Asked by Carlson to define *modernism*, Popenoe spoke of "hedonistic individualism" as the pervasive social problem. Americans have espoused a strong individualism since the founding of the nation, but in the past this individualism has been wrapped around commitments to family, religion, and small communities. Now, however, as the containing forces have disappeared, individualism has become much more self-oriented and narcissistic. Popenoe saw this regrettable cultural trend in every modern society, whether organized as a capitalist free market or as a socialist welfare state.

The capitalist profit motive, Day pointed out, could not account for the high rates for divorce and abortion in the Soviet Union. Soviet authorities tightly censor TV broadcasts while presiding over an economy that offers no incentives for family dissolution. Divorcing couples find it almost impossible to find a new apartment. Still the Soviet divorce rate runs high.

Sympathetic to Douglas' antistatist arguments, Mattox interpreted the current failure of the underclass to respond to job opportunities — mentioned earlier by Neely — as evidence that the growth of the welfare state has fundamentally affected human behavior. The development of the welfare system has not produced the desired effects. In Mattox's view, any dismantling of the welfare state would encourage greater individual responsibility for decisions in marriage and childbearing.

Renewing his attack upon modernism, Douglas agreed with Popenoe about the importance of hedonism in reshaping society. But modernism also springs from the belief that through rational science people have now transcended human nature, gaining superiority over earlier generations. Based upon the assumption that individual happiness should define man's goal in life, modernism repudiates all traditions, all ancient common sense governing love, intimacy, motherhood. This tremendous cultural break with the past is slowly communicated to the broader population through formal education. Douglas gloomily predicted that worse lay in store, as the modernist mentality justifies even greater intrusions by the state into the family.

Smith dissented from Douglas' assessment, arguing that the decline in the family reflected the consequences of industrialization, not simply changes in social values. Invoking the work of Kingsley Davis, Smith suggested that industrialization created internal contradictions in the way that it forced men out of the household as breadwinners, while assigning women the role of homemakers. In the passage to the egalitarian family, people are recognizing that the normative order governing the old system does not work very well. Men and women are accordingly trying to make adaptations. Smith sensed a widespread agreement among Americans — liberal and conservative — that the family is suffering, that divorce and illegitimacy are undesirable. Yet he feared that anti-statist ideology would prevent the formation of coalitions that might do something practical. Smith held conservatives responsible for a failure to alleviate family problems. After all, a conservative administration had governed the nation the last eight years, while the business elite exercised remarkable power and authority. Smith expressed particular frustration with business leaders who profess conservative views about the family, but will do nothing practical — like making part-time work easier for women — to help families.

Fleming protested that the Reagan Administration did not represent the aspirations of traditionalist conservatives. Christensen agreed, complaining that the label "conservatism" is not very helpful when used to speak of an unthinking alliance between promoters of big business and people concerned about the family. Despite common usage, Christensen thought it a mistake to call the defenders of big business "conservative."

A cultural drift toward materialism, Christensen suggested, could explain the high levels of family dissolution in both the United States and the European welfare states. He cited a recent survey of high school seniors in which researchers found an inverse correlation between financial aspiration and future commitment to family life. The seniors who cared most about money and getting ahead cared least about marriage and family.

As a legal expert on product liability, Neely had enough experi-ence with the nation's business elite to clear them of blame for intentionally weakening the family. On the whole, he reported, these business elite are decent people. Yet capitalism has weak-ened the family by separating man from his means of production, so destroying the viability of the extended family. Adult children now rarely live close to their parents. As a largely progressive force, the business community would like to make life better for the family, but Neely worried about possible unintended consequences. For example, if policymakers change the employment structure to help women find part-time work or day care, do they then create an economic system in which part-time work and day care become desperately necessary in order to pay the "social charges" imposed by such a system?

Countering earlier remarks by Popenoe and Douglas, Neely discounted hedonism as an overrated cause of family dissolution. By providing superb medical care, low infant mortality, and long life, modern capitalism has caused changes in people's normative structure, often against their will. Neely saw this normative shift especially in childbearing decisions. Many of the American upper class now believe bearing a child creates a deficit for the world. Even among Catholics who would like to have five or six children, many couples restrain themselves, because their secular normali-zation overwhelms their religious normalization.

The decision to restrict childbearing reflects more than econom-ics, Carlson reminded conference participants. He recalled a recent study of Mexican Americans which found much lower fertility in households where English was spoken than in those where Spanish was used, even though researchers made statistical allowance for household income.

As the only bureaucrat in attendance, Cabaniss felt that confer-ence participants had not yet bashed bureaucrats enough. She suggested that a number of Federal policies could be indicted for subsidizing the retreat from marriage. She singled out for particu-lar attention the family-planning program operating out of her own office. To the extent that the program subsidizes sexual activity outside of marriage, the family-planning program may in fact be viewed as helping to advance the retreat from marriage. Respond-ing to the tone of Douglas' paper, Cabaniss stressed that an apocalyptic outlook is not warranted so long as good people avail themselves of the privileges of representative government, so countering the ambitions of special-interest groups.

Provoked by Neely's earlier remarks, Kasun repudiated any type of population control inspired by a vision of people populating out of control like rats in a tub or fruit flies in a bottle. Human beings are rational, she insisted, especially in a true free market which gives people the best incentives in the world for not over-populating. But when the welfare system removes the controls of the market by paying teenage girls to set up their own households, it is folly to blame capitalism for the resulting decline in family life, especially in the black family. The state has further hurt the black family through the enforcement of minimum-wage statutes, which artificially shut young black men out of labor opportunities.

Popenoe still could not accept the bleakness of the picture painted by Douglas. If the world has reached such a desperate position, why is it that in the United States or Sweden or other advanced societies people appear quite satisfied, even with their marriages? People are not saying that society is going to hell in a handbasket, nor are they saying they would have preferred to live fifty years ago. In recent years, the developed nations have seen a tremendous decrease in inequality, as more people than ever before have attained the good life. Even the threat of war no longer clouds the horizon.

Capitalism had not received sufficient scrutiny to satisfy Schoen, who thought that the capitalist motivation for weakening the family might not lie simply in the desire to sell more and more goods to more and more households. Capitalists also seek to enlarge the labor force by bringing very large numbers of women into paid employment. This movement of women into paid labor has effected tremendous changes in the family and in society. As people look at their changed circumstances, they are making new choices. But they are not especially happy about their choices — in divorce, in abortion, in cohabitation. Schoen did not see much chance for improving the situation simply by relying on human nature, since human nature acts within a particular environment and economic circumstances. However, the larger social interest in the welfare of children could offer hope. By seeking the welfare of children, Schoen thought it possible to help people to overcome self-interest and to make socially desirable choices.

As the third session of the conference drew to a close, Vinovskis voiced regret that because of the focus upon the ultimate costs of the retreat from family, participants had not explored the more immediate, short-term costs of the retreat from marriage. Without an examination of that topic, Vinovskis feared the conference would have little impact upon current debates.

Douglas acknowledged the existence of a huge literature, generally skewed to the left in his opinion, assessing the supposed costs and benefits of family dissolution. Mentioned briefly in his paper, John Bowlby had particularly researched the fundamental issues of how insecurity and an inadequate sense of self result from the breaking of the mother-child bond. In his book *Sexual Suicide*, reissued in a second edition as *Men and Marriage*, George Gilder catalogued the social deficiencies of fatherless families. Yet the cultural bias against any nonmodernist perspective on family questions may be seen in the fact that although Simon and Schuster had earned considerable profits from the first edition, they refused to publish the second edition, forcing Gilder to take it to a minor publisher. In any case, Douglas thought it crucial to examine first things first, not secondary cost-benefit questions. Rebutting Popenoe's contention that people are not that unhappy in their current circumstances, Douglas compared current circumstances to those in the 1920's when F. Scott Fitzgerald was writing *The Great Gatsby*, when everything was wondrous and buzzing. But in the 1930's, everyone crashed, including Fitzgerald, who spiraled into alcoholism and early death. What is it going to be like in the future, Douglas wondered, when the bills come due? Even at the present, Americans are suffering great emotional distress caused by divorce, family dissolution, and failed relationships. "Are people more unhappy today than in the past?" he asked. "You damn well bet they are!" he thundered. This unhappiness is manifest in the high rates of drug addiction, suicide, murder, and rape. Women now fear rape in areas where the crime was virtually unknown twenty or thirty years ago.

Opening the final session of the conference, Christensen characterized his paper as more literary than sociological — as a dark and even apocalyptic vision of the future in which family disintegration appears as part of a broader cultural malaise. As symptom and cause of that malaise, modern utopianism figures as a particularly potent foe of the family. Adapting an imaginative polarity borrowed from Peter Medewar, Christensen identified an antithesis between Utopia and Eden, as depicted in Genesis. As described critically by Yevgeny Zamyatin and sympathetically by B.F. Skinner, the utopian project consists of improving upon Genesis, of fixing the mistake made by Adam and Eve, so engineering a way out of the Fall. Because of the desire to deny the constraints of a post-Edenic world, New Left philosopher Herbert Marcuse discouraged philosophic or theological contemplation of death, because such contemplation stifles the utopian impulse. Drawing upon the research of Philippe Aries, Christensen noted that — partly because of utopian aspiration — many Americans and Western Europeans live in the myth of immortality, refusing to consider or discuss death. This death denial makes a difference for marriage and childbearing: immortals, after all, do not need to bear children. George Orwell had warned that as Christianity fades, the temptation grows strong to take consolation in some optimistic illusion. Looking at the same cultural development, the critic T.E. Hulme complained of "spilt religion," as faith is displaced to new objects. This spilt religion, Christensen observed, makes people impatient with the post-Edenic realities of adversity, sin, and death. He reiterated J. Hillis Miller's observation that in later 19th-century fiction the search for the ideal mate replaces the search for God — another instance of spilt religion. Christensen conjectured that one of the reasons marriages fail is that people now want to marry a perfect mate, a god or goddess.

To the question, What are we to do? Christensen offered only skepticism for global solutions. Individuals should marry, love their spouses, take care of their children, act decently in their neighborhood. He cautioned against further expansion of the state, fearing that government solutions to the problems of family dissolution would make matters worse in the long run.

In his prepared response, Popenoe placed Christensen's paper in the tradition of Pitirim Sorokin, one of the social theorists he had admired most earlier in his career. Sorokin was in many respects a supreme conservative who believed that social change is cyclical, with each cycle ending in a cultural crisis, leading eventually to a new cycle. He thought that Western civilization in the 20th century was in an end-of-cycle cultural crisis, predicting that after much turmoil society would be renewed through a religious revival and a new set of cultural values. Popenoe still found much of Sorokin's perspective appealing, agreeing that we are in a cultural crisis, evident in the retreat from marriage and the family. But despite this fundamental agreement, Popenoe took issue with Christensen about the desirability — and possibility — of restoring the traditional family in which the husband is the breadwinner and the wife is a full-time homemaker. Popenoe conceded that the movement of married women into the labor force has created some difficulties for women, men, children, and the family. Yet he was convinced that restoring the traditional family (after all, a rather recent social invention in history) was not a realistic social goal. Most women in the modern world do not wish to turn back the clock. Popenoe urged a continued fight to preserve the nuclear family, but that family should be egalitarian, permitting women to combine paid employment with family life and freeing women from subordination to men in the home.

Popenoe also rejected Christensen's argument that the family could be strengthened by pushing back the welfare state. He reiterated his observation that among developed nations family decline is most pronounced in the United States and in Sweden, although Sweden has the strongest welfare state in the industrial world and the U.S. the weakest. Clearly, he reasoned, the welfare state is not to blame for family decline, at least no more so than free-market capitalism in America. It is a cruel irony, Popenoe remarked, that giving help to broken homes may to a small extent cause more homes to break up. But it is simply cruel not to provide help when so many homes are breaking up.

Popenoe conceded that the solution to the malaise in family life might lie beyond economics or politics. The fundamental cause of the recent retreat from marriage probably is a profound moral change, a change from an ethic of social commitment to one of self-fulfillment. This ethical shift is tied as much to modern capitalism as it is to the modern welfare state — and transcends both. Are there any grounds for optimism? Surveying the last twenty five years, Popenoe saw not only a pronounced decline in family life, but also many positive developments. For example, there is far less inequality in the industrialized world than in the past, and war between the major world powers has grown unlikely. Are there reasons for anticipating a new cultural cycle bringing marriage and family back into the cultural center? Popenoe was encouraged that despite their headlong rush toward self-fulfillment, the overwhelming majority of young people still regard marriage and child-rearing as major life goals. Although the achievement of these goals has been impeded by the pursuit of individualism and by contemporary affluence, their persistence is based on a deep-seated human need. It is reasonable to speculate, therefore, that in time this basic need will come to the fore, radical individualism will be contained, and a new cultural cycle will commence.

Turning from the broader cultural questions to a concrete issue, Neely wanted help in formulating an opinion about day care. Should the government act to ensure quality day care because it may alleviate the terrible cultural deprivation of children from broken homes? Or would government subsidy of day care merely exacerbate family woes pushing America closer to the Swedish model?

Popenoe responded that it probably would be best for the children of the American underclass to receive substantial day care beginning at a young age. The Head Start program in particular has won endorsement from almost everyone as perhaps the one success of the government's anti-poverty efforts. In Sweden, on the other hand, child-development experts generally encourage parents to be at home for the first three years of a child's life. Swedish parental leave allows a mother or father to stay home for fifteen months at about 90 percent of salary — paid for by the state and the employer. This parental leave will soon be lengthened to 18 months and perhaps eventually to 3 years, in keeping with the recommendation of child-development experts. By the third year, most Swedish children have entered day care, as their care-taking parent (usually the mother) often returns to work, part-time at first.

Cabaniss, on the other hand, cited "The Head Start Evaluation Synthesis and Utilization Project" released by the U.S. Department of Health & Human Services in 1985, which reported that while Head Start may have an immediate and short-term effect on academic performance, its effect disappears by the time children enter the second or third grade. By that point, children who were placed in Head Start do no better in school than children from comparable backgrounds who were not.

Given the reported shortage of day care, however, Smith still thought that day-care policy deserved scrutiny. Theory may predict that some day-care initiatives might cause the decline of a particu-

lar kind of family, although the evidence is scanty. Yet what of the
welfare of the children themselves if government does nothing to
regulate day care?

Shifting attention to a more fundamental question, Smith asked
Christensen whether any cultural force other than religion could
provide people with values permitting family life. Christensen
responded that inherited traditions and economic supports could
help sustain family life, but that all such cultural reinforcements
become hollow over time without spiritual conviction. Parting
company with Douglas, Christensen judged the Victorian era as an
age of hollowness and unthinking conformity. Nearer our own time,
he recalled a survey taken during the 1950's of women graduates
of Smith, Vassar, or one of the other elite women's colleges. Asked
about their life goals, these women spoke of highly domestic
futures: they wished to marry, have children, make a home. But
then came the second question. Why? Most of the women could not
give a reason. Their family commitments were fundamentally
hollow. Christensen hoped he had not given the impression he
wanted to go back to the 1950's, when strong family life was largely
a cut-flower illusion.

Also addressing Smith's question about possible sources of
values, Douglas noted that the Japanese are not religious in the
traditional Western sense, yet their family ties remain the strongest seen in any developed nation. Many developments, including
practical changes and the adoption of new technologies, cause the
hollowness, the decline in commitment to values, seen in recent
decades. This decline has been fostered by the secularization of the
Western World, seen most strikingly in the United States, the
Western nation historically most Christian — and still so, although
Christianity is fast fading in America, especially among the intellectuals. One consequence of this secularization is that relatively
few Americans now regard marriage as sacred, as an institution
ordained of God. Cut off from their roots by modernism, Americans
today have no sense of sacredness for anything, although they do
have a real sense of loss.

Mattox joined Popenoe in identifying the defense of the nuclear
family as a primary social goal, yet he remained unconvinced that
women en masse desire an egalitarian family rather than a traditional one. He supposed that the vast majority of women want
something between the two extremes. Consequently, Mattox could

not support massive government support for day-care programs which socially engineer an egalitarian lifestyle and foreclose options for women preferring a traditional lifestyle. In Mattox's solution, the tax burden on families would be reduced, so empowering people to make their own decisions about how to order their family lives. Government should not engineer people's domestic lives.

Popenoe agreed, noting that when in Sweden he expresses more concern about lifestyle engineering. American social policies, however, are still far different from Sweden's.

Do the traditional marriages that feminists so criticize really entail very much involuntary tyranny? Neely wondered. In his own experience, most breadwinning husbands exercise no power in their homes except that agreed upon by their wives.

As a classicist, Fleming similarly questioned the accuracy of standard accounts of patriarchal fathers in ancient Greece, where women were supposedly reduced to colorless creatures of no status. How is it, then, that Greek drama is filled with such passionate, colorful women — wonderful mothers, domineering bullies, witty and amusing rebels, sex-crazed fiends, even terrible murderers? In any society, Fleming suggested, the men may be officially in charge, but deeper investigation will reveal a more complicated arrangement of power, worked out in individual homes.

Cabaniss joined the small chorus questioning the supposed subordination of women in marriage. Though herself unmarried, Cabaniss' personal observation led her to believe that women are typically in total control of home life and that it is perhaps men who are subordinated in that setting. Society's problem may not be those of a patriarchal society, but may instead be those of a matriarchal society in which men are increasingly regarded as economic providers only and are, therefore, detached from child-rearing and other domestic activities.

On Cabaniss' theme of the dominance of women and passivity of men, Nock observed that sociologists frequently speak of the powerlessness of women, because they adopt a male model of power as the ability to have one's say even against the wishes of others. But if power is defined instead as the ability to influence beliefs or affect behavior, then women can hardly be tyrannized in most traditional families, where their influence is generally much greater than males.

Likewise inspired by Cabaniss, Day observed that for some time the popular culture of media, entertainment, and cartoons has inculcated a mythology of the irrelevant male, the Dagwood Bumstead character who is a bungling, stumbling person who is amusing but unimportant. He noted a study of cartoons that appeared in the *Saturday Evening Post* over a 50 year period, consistently portraying fathers (but not mothers) as humorous buffoons likely to crash into fish bowls or put frogs in the dryer. This consistent portrayal of men as irrelevant and detached seems hard to justify in light of recent research based upon observations of 60,000-70,000 children in public places in twenty diverse countries in which men are generally with their children — whenever work permits — performing essentially the same kinds of tasks as mothers. Could it be that American men somehow maintain their masculine image as John Wayne figures, protectors of their families, by convincing themselves that if they ever moved into the domestic realm they would certainly foul it up? In any case, the image of the irrelevant male has probably made it easier to accept the mother-state-child household as an acceptable replacement for the father-mother-child family. Day feared that his young sons might not understand their role as father, either at the mythological level or the real level.

Douglas could see a fairly consistent cross-cultural relationship between the sexes. In virtually all civilizations, men do the outside work, go on the long trips, do the hunting and trading over long distances; women typically trade in the local market and run the household. In domestic matters, women manage matters day to day, while men hold ultimate authority for larger decisions about such things as buying a house or car — though such decisions are usually made with the wife's consent. Simply as a matter of human nature, men are bigger and stronger and look more impressive and frightening — especially to children. Although there have always been a few women leaders, Douglas judged it symptomatic of a decadent and wimpish society such as Britain that a woman would rise to the top as an "iron Maggie."

Echoing Day's earlier remarks, Carlson observed that even in the 1950's, the heyday of domesticity, television often depicted fathers as irrelevant bunglers. In the classic *Leave It to Beaver*, for instance, Ward Cleaver appears as a pretty pathetic character who shows up occasionally to clean his golf clubs. His position in the home is vague and somewhat bizarre.

On the other hand, Neely could not think of too many TV programs that focused on women. Women do not typically engage in tasks that create opportunities for personal heroism in the struggle between good and evil.

Redirecting discussion, Carlson asked who viewed the future with optimism rather than with the pessimism voiced by Christensen and Douglas. Although unable to view the troubling trends in family life with optimism, Nock did see the average person as freer today than the average version of 200, 400, 600, or 800 years ago. In theory, the growth of the state should mean greater social control, but so far the freedom of the individual continues to increase. Perhaps this growth of individual freedom is part of the problem.

In classical political theory, Carlson observed, freedom was defined as an individual prerogative. He wondered whether the retreat from marriage did not reflect this greater feeling of individual freedom, freedom from responsibility, freedom from children, even freedom through divorce from an unsatisfactory spouse. The culture no longer condemns the man who divorces his wife and disclaims responsibility for his children. The government has established programs to pick up the pieces after such a decision.

Nock agreed that the increasing freedom of individuals had helped cause a retreat from the family. Glenn's decision to focus on personal *satisfaction* as the key to understanding the cultural meaning of marriage illustrated, in Nock's view, how individual freedom had changed contemporary attitudes toward marriage.

Still, Vinovskis did not find life two or three hundred years ago attractive. He conceded a preference for some of the strengths of family life in past centuries, yet he still would not have wanted to live under the kind of control parents had over their children in the 17th century, when parents arranged the marriages for sons and daughters. Vinovskis found the material circumstances of past centuries even less acceptable, since such circumstances meant high mortality and few opportunities for economic or political advancement. Nor could he feel any enthusiasm for the 19th-century auction system of welfare in which people were put up for bid for someone to take care of them. In short, Vinovskis was quite glad to have been born in this rather than an earlier century. He cautioned other participants not to romanticize the family life of the past.

Vinovskis did not put much stock in Douglas' warnings of impending doom. As far back as the 1820's and 1830's, some voices warned that the family was falling apart, society headed for big trouble. Although these jeremiads may contain elements of truth, they can no longer evoke deep anxieties when repeated long enough.

Sounding a note of optimism, Mattox took hope in new developments in computer technology and telecommunications. In these new technologies, he saw the possibility for men and women to perform stimulating, remunerative work at home, so solving many of the problems dividing the home and the workplace. The computer revolution may permit a resurgence in family life, at least among the significant number of Americans who still want that.

Neely took heart from a different development, namely the rethinking of family questions in magazines that draw heavily from leftist contributors. People who fifteen years ago advocated autonomy, childlessness, and sexual liberation are now admitting error as they look for something in between traditionalism and radical liberation. For instance, in their recent reactions against pornography, feminists are in part repudiating the notion — fashionable in the early 1970's — that sexual liberation for men gives sexual liberation for women, too. Perhaps the cultural trends against the family will prove self-adjusting over time.

In the shifts in ideological coalitions, Smith saw evidence of the unfairness of caricatures of the leftists as good-intentioned, but ignorant — even evil. This myth of evil leftists obscured the reality of people readjusting past judgments when confronted with facts.

Unsure of the prophet's mantle given him by Vinovskis, Douglas nonetheless predicted that the current plateau period would be followed by a worldwide economic depression — and perhaps by wars and revolutions. More generally, he anticipated a cultural crisis of the sort described by Sorokin. Despite these gloomy forecasts, Douglas remained optimistic about human nature over the long run. After crises, people always put life back together again, he observed.

Returning to Smith's earlier questions about whether family life can be founded on anything but religious conviction, Christensen recalled the words of Malachi at the end of the Old Testament: Malachi promises that the Lord would turn the hearts of the children to the fathers and the fathers to the children, warning that if this did not happen, the earth would be smitten with a curse. (See Mal. 4:5, 6.) In light of these verses, Christensen felt that a reflective appreciation for parents, grandparents, and ancestors could fortify family life, even if this appreciation could not be expressed with any doctrinal rigor.

To focus the discussion during the closing minutes of the conference, Carlson reminded participants of the four questions defining the agenda: What is happening to family life? Why is it happening? What are the consequences? What, if anything, should we do about it? Although he did not believe the group had reached any consensus, Carlson identified several major themes emerging in the debate. First, has the growth of the state caused the decline of the family — or is capitalism to blame? Or do both the burgeoning state and unrestrained capitalism reflect some deeper cultural force undermining marriage? Perhaps, as Popenoe suggested, the problem reflects a long-term shift from social commitment to self-fulfillment — from *Gemeinschaft* to *Gesellschaft*, from tradition to modernity. Since all present regarded family dissolution as a problem, Carlson asked for specific suggestions to strengthen families.

Neely urged other conference participants to discard their ideological baggage in order to make deals in practical politics. As part of an aggressive strategy for changing the propaganda model for family issues, Neely recommended writing for *The New Republic*, *The Nation*, or the *Atlantic Monthly*, so reaching audiences yet to be convinced. No need to preach to the converted by writing for conservative magazines. Neely dismissed as unachievable proposals for dismantling the bureaucratic state or for reviving religions, particularly Christianity, that have been repudiated historically. What might and should be done is to convince people that the retreat from marriage — either by divorce or by failure to marry in the first place — is disastrous for society and for individuals.

Taking a darker view, Day could see only tragic resolutions for some of the disputed issues. If, for instance, legal abortion continues, then Americans will abort enough children every seven or eight years to have populated a city the size of Los Angeles. Yet if abortion is limited or outlawed, many children will be born into lives of great difficulty. Similarly, to oppose divorce may mean keeping people in abusive, unhappy marriages. Day confessed that he needed to make some hard choices personally about how to resolve the tensions between individualism and family commitment. Yet he refused to feel powerless when confronting these questions. As a professor who had taught 200-300 students a year for 15 years, he felt he had influenced many people. By fighting for the adoption of a general-education course on the family at Washington State University, Day hoped to exert yet greater influence.

Day's proposal for a required family course provoked a skeptical response from Glenn, who feared what some professors might do with such a course. Carlson chimed in, noting that ideologies invariably creep into parent and family education.

Cabaniss pointed out that since the feminist movement and the sexual revolution have powerfully influenced the retreat from marriage and since that retreat has hurt women and children the most, any improvement can best start with women. If women universally — including those in the inner city — refused to accept men's irresponsible behavior, births would not occur out of wedlock, nor would a husband be able to leave his wife for another woman.

Children should define the focus for public policy on family issues, Vinovskis argued. Next, he advocated strategies for helping disadvantaged groups. To help such groups, policymakers need to address the redistribution of resources. In particular, public policy must enforce a father's responsibilities for child support, an issue neglected at this conference. Yet Vinovskis was encouraged by the frequency with which conference participants alluded to history or other cultures. Most policymakers, he complained, suppose that a look back at the 1970's gives them an historical perspective, failing to understand the longer-term development of many of our assumptions. In Washington, where people cannot remember what happened two years ago, policymakers reinvent things over and over again.

Popenoe enumerated four specific measures to strengthen the family. First, he joined Carlson in advocating tax breaks for families with children. Americans now widely accept the welfare-state benefits given senior citizens, yet many strongly resist any new benefit for children. Policy in the U.S. must begin to shift away from the elderly toward children. Second, Popenoe advocated parental leave. Describing his daughters as typical of many young women today, he spoke of their desire for professional careers while still having children. Parental leave would help them to have both. Third, Popenoe called for wider provision of high quality child care. Fourth, agreeing with Vinovskis, Popenoe endorsed a national strategy for locating fathers and compelling payment of child support. Despite the practical difficulties of such a policy, its enactment would send a strong signal.

But Glenn predicted enforcement of such a child-support strategy would prove simply impossible among the black underclass, partly because so many young black men are dead, in jail, or otherwise unavailable by their late 20's. Although Vinovskis disputed his assessment, Glenn did not see responsible fatherhood as a viable solution for the black underclass.

Christensen added tougher divorce laws to the list of policy recommendations. He cited a study in the late 1970's in which researchers discovered that two years after the event, two-thirds of divorced men and women expressed serious second thoughts about their decision to divorce. Easy divorce may not be a benefit even for many who think they want it.

With Popenoe, Smith thought that public attitudes could be influenced by enactment of a policy for tracking down financially irresponsible fathers. Such a policy would send the message that society collectively values the well-being of children and so favors financial responsibility of fathers. In this way, the policy might — despite failures in its implementation — help shape prevailing attitudes about the long-term consequences of sexual behavior and about the duties of fatherhood.

Advancing a libertarian proposal, Douglas suggested that couples be allowed to negotiate their own marriage contract, establishing their own terms of dissolution. In his view, almost all intelligent and sane young women (and many of the men) would insist upon stern conditions for dissolution. By enacting "no fault" statutes for divorce, legislators retroactively abrogated — without due process — the rights of married women, especially older married women. If individuals could determine their own wedding contracts, terms for dissolution would probably become sterner.

Many states already permit such prenuptial negotiation, Neely reported. His own state of West Virginia enforces such prenuptial agreements, not only in second marriages where such contracts protect property which a spouse wishes to leave to children of a first marriage, but also in first marriages where the spouses have chosen to set their own terms for dissolution. The courts have regarded such contracts as presumptively valid, permitting judicial discretion to change the terms only if the contract is old — say 30 years old — before it becomes operative. When judges do change the terms of long-standing prenuptial agreements, they act only to protect people from their own past stupidity. If, for instance, a 62-year-old woman had pledged in a prenuptial agreement signed 30 or 40 years ago that she would ask for nothing if the marriage failed, the court probably would not enforce that agreement.

Carlson reminded participants of the novelty of state regulation of marriage. Until relatively late in Western history, churches, not the state, regulated marriages. Exercising a chairman's prerogative, Carlson stressed the economic independence of the home in giving his own policy prescription for strengthening the family. In order to defend itself against destructive cultural forces, the family must find ways of rebuilding the home economy in its broadest sense, reclaiming some of the functions that the family has shed in the past, bringing into the home productive activities ranging from computer programming to handicrafts. Although such a strategy depends upon personal commitment, policymakers can help by easing zoning regulations, labor laws, and other barriers to home production.

Echoing Carlson's theme, Mattox saw in the home economy the possibility for people to spend more time with spouses and children. Besides making it easier for people to live near extended families, working at home would permit the rebuilding of community life. At present, the workplace provides the only semblance of community in the lives of most people, who rarely do anything significant with their neighbors. As more people do their work at home, they will naturally rely more upon their neighbors, fostering greater community feeling.

Asked by Popenoe for evidence that work actually is shifting to the home, Mattox noted that just last year IBM instituted a policy enabling many employees, particularly young women, to work out of their homes on an experimental project. A number of insurance, communication, and financial firms — including Aetna, Travelers, American Express, and AT&T — have likewise moved in this direction. For these companies, work at home will remain an employer-employee relationship. Mattox hoped to see more home-based entrepreneurial enterprises, including some in which husband and wife work together.

Sounding a cautionary note, Popenoe cited studies depicting home work as a double bind and tremendous role conflict for women. He recalled interviews of women working at home with children playing around their feet, with life for some of these children much worse than in a day-care center.

Mattox agreed that in many cases a mother working at home would need substitute care for her children. Home work performed in the 19th century was largely physical labor that did not require intellectual concentration, so allowing those who were involved to look after children. Contemporary work on a computer does require intellectual concentration. Perhaps a mother engaged in such work could find child care by turning to her extended family or her husband. In any case, solutions to such problems ought not be imposed by ivory-tower policymakers but ought to be worked out by individual families given the freedom to make their own decisions.

Convinced that all present had voiced their views, Carlson expressed appreciation to everyone for an illuminating conversation.

Index—Names and Topics

ELIZABETH TOWN COMMUNITY COLLEGE
Elizabethtown, KY 42701